# PUTSCH

# PUTSCH

## The Diary
## Three Days That Collapsed The Empire

### Introduction by
### Boris Yeltsin

*Translated From Russian*

MOSAIC PRESS

OAKVILLE-NEW YORK-LONDON

CANADIAN CATALOGUING IN PUBLICATION DATA

Putsch : three days that collapsed the empire : the diary

Translated from the Russian.
ISBN 0-88962-509-3 (bound)    0-88962-522-0 (pbk.)

1. Soviet Union - History - Attempted coup, 1991 - Sources.

DK292.P88 1992   947.085'4    C92-094673-9

Published by MOSAIC PRESS, P.O. Box 1032, Oakville, Ontario, L6J 5E9, Canada. Offices and warehouse at 1252 Speers Road, Units #1&2, Oakville, Ontario, L6L 5N9, Canada.

Mosaic Press acknowledges the assistance of the Canada Council and the Ontario Arts Council in support of its publishing programme.

Copyright © 1992, Progress Publishers/IPI
Design by Patty Gallinger
Typset by Jackie Ernst
Printed and bound in Canada
Translated from Russian, originally published in 1991

ISBN 0-88962-509-3 HC        0-88962-522-0 PB

MOSAIC PRESS:
In Canada:
        MOSAIC PRESS, 1252 Speers Road, Units #1&2, Oakville, Ontario, L6L 5N9, P.O. Box 1032, Oakville, Ontario L6J 5E9, Canada.

In the United States:
        Distributed to the trade in the United States by: National Book Network, Inc., 4720-A Boston Way, Lanham, MD, 20706, USA

# TABLE OF CONTENTS

# INTRODUCTION

### B.N.YELTSIN
### PRESIDENT OF RUSSIA

*The August Coup Was Not Accidental*

The August 19-22, 1991 coup was not accidental. In fact, it happened as a natural result of the policies that has been implemented in the country for some time. For a long time now in the USSR there existed a major crisis of power which became deeper and deeper.

For many, many months, the leadership of the USSR had in fact been acting like the leadership of China, without a clear political direction, pronouncing right slogans, but doing nothing practically to achieve the realization of these slogans.

The implementation of the reform agenda had been entrusted to organs of the state that were totalitarian in their very nature. It seemed that everything was being done to save the state/party structures from their inevitable destruction.

The most important positions in the reform process had actually been entrusted to people who were, "de facto", leaders of reactionary forces. This approach had led to a deep crisis, to a total disorganization of life in the entire country.

Once again, the elementary political truth had been confirmed: reformers and reactionaries, supporters of dictatorship and democracy, oppressors of freedom and defenders of freedom could not possibly all go in one direction.

Since last year, republics began playing an active role in the country. The more conservative and entrenched Union (administrative) structures, which were known to oppose everything new, assumed sharply confrontational position towards these initiatives from the republics. A de-facto "cold war" had been going on between the centre and the republics for about a year.

The Union (administrative) structures could not comprehend and appreciate that the newly found sovereignty of the republics, including the former autonomous republics within these republics, was not due to the 'intrigues'of democrats, but was in fact a genuine and objective tendency of our time.

There were hopes that the Congress and the USSR Supreme Soviet would be able to begin a general reconstruction of the centre. These bodies were allotted significant authority and could have had considerable influence upon the renewal of union structures.

Alas, it did not happen! During the days of the Putsch the country did not have an effective supreme legislative authority, nor did it have a parliament. The hands of the junta were free. The Supreme Soviet, because of its idleness, guaranteed the junta the most favourable conditions for a coup. If we are to speak in general terms, the Union centre, had basically remained unchanged.

It fell hopelessly behind the country and ceased to understand the very processes it had been going through. The Party and the bureaucracy, or Partocracy, whose attitude towards reforms was well known, continued to play a decisive role in the centre. And when it became clear that the country was finally coming out from under the monopolistic control of the supreme party-state structures, it decided to use the last resort - violence - against millions of citizens, against its own country. The Partocracy decided to use force to turn the country backwards.

In evaluating the causes for the Putsch I cannot overlook the role of the President of the country.

His inconsistency in implementing reforms, his indecisiveness and, at times, capitulation when faced with the aggressive attacks of the partocracy - all these factors created favourable conditions for the 'revenge' of the totalitarian system. I don't think Mikhail Sergeevich knew the true character of Yanayeb, Kruchkov, Pugo, Yazov and the others.

Let us remember that as early as January 1991 the country began to feel uneasy about the President's sharp turn to the right. One by one, democratic achievements were given up, the oppressive role of the KGB was increased, the role of the military in political decision making was legitimized, controls over the sources of mass information were made more rigid. Pavlov, and not Yavlinsky, was sent to the London meeting of the

Group of Seven by the President despite the fact that the results of Pavlov's economic policies were disastrous and were painfully felt by all the people of the country.

Yes, today we have the right to ask Gorbachev some tough questions. I want to underline: to ask tough questions, not to settle the score. After the coup, the country as a whole, especially Russia has changed. The President has also changed. He found strength in himself to reevaluate many things. I, for instance, personally trust Mikhail Sergeevich today much more than even 3 weeks after the Putsch.

The meaning and the future existence of our institutions under our new conditions lies in the agreements and co-ordination of the republics' activities. The coup ruined the signing of the Union Treaty but could not evaporate the republics' aspirations to build up a new union. The destruction of the totalitarian system became irreversible, but the deep desire for new voluntary, equal relations between republics were not actualized then. It was this desire for new relations that has withstood the chaos and anarchy in our country, while the supreme state organs were demoralized and inactive. And today, it is the republics that are the main source of stability. Aiming to crush them will only push the country towards catastrophe.

The situation in our country is so complex that we need radical decisions and urgent measures which are clear to everyone.

Here are some propositions for concrete actions:

First: preservation of a single economic zone of the country. Republics, (practically all of them) are now ready to conclude an economic union in order to ensure the normal function of the economy and assure peoples' livelihood during this transitional period. Of course, today we also require measures for survival in regards to food.

Second: creation of a system of free co-operation of sovereign states, based upon the existence of different forms of interstate relations. And here, we have to agree that there may be independent republics, which would insist on confederation - not federation - which would insist upon associate membership and an economic union, but would nevertheless be part of a single system.

Third: preservation of our military forces with some ultimate control of our nuclear arsenals. Military reform is needed. Russia, in its turn, would guarantee the preservation of the army's nuclear potential. Thus, the nuclear potential would not fall into either "hawks" nor "extremists" hands. For this, already today, special structures are being created. At the same time we are in favour of a considerable reduction in defence spending. The level of spending should be defined by two criteria: defence sufficiency and strengthening of the social protection of servicemen.

Fourth: implementation of strong guarantees of human rights all across the country, the Republics and all territory. Russia confirms its support of all relevant treaties it has signed in respect to this question. It will defend the interests of the Russian republic. Russia will build relations with sovereign states only on the basis of equality, good neighbourliness, mutual benefit and non-interference in each others internal affairs. The Russian state which chooses democracy and freedom will never be an empire. I will never be "a big brother" or a "younger brother". It will be equal among equals. It is short-sighted from a political point of view, immoral from an ethical point of view, and foolish from a man's point of view, to waste time and cling to old dogmas and ideals that were and are preached by some.

The whole world today not only sympathises with us and followed very closely the events of August 19,20,21, 1991 but is also ready to give us real support, especially in a complex period of transition.

Finally, we ourselves must also accept our responsibility before our own people and before all of humanity for our deeds and our future.


B.N. Yeltsin

# FOREWORD

## INTERVIEW BETWEEN ALEXANDER AVELICHEV AND PROFESSOR HOWARD ASTER

Q:   Please indicate how and when you decided that Progress Publishers should undertake to prepare a book on the Putsch?

It was in the early morning of August 20th, 1991. I was driving with my Literary Director of Progress Publishers in my car. We were heading towards our offices at Progress in the center of Moscow. We were thinking that we were in the midst of an astonishing period, a vital period of our lives and the life of our country. We did not know how it would resolve itself. Nobody knew at that time. But we knew that we should not allow a new mythology to be created five or ten years after the events that were now taking place around us. We realized that we were obliged to take notes and prepare records about the events that were unfolding that very day. That is why we decided there and then - the morning of August 20, 1991 - that we would undertake to prepare a book, a real diary, of the events of the Putsch.

We had no idea at that time if the book would be published in two years, three years or five years. But we were convinced that we had to collect all the facts, to document all the eye-witness accounts of people so that, at some point in time in the future, a book would, indeed, be published.

We arrived in the Progress offices in the morning of August 20, 1991. I received a phone call from the Director of the news agency, POSTFACTUM. I suggested to him that we meet. He came to our offices. I knew by then, of course, that POSTFACTUM and RIA, the Russian Independent Agency, the two most important, new and independent news agencies, were hard at work collecting and distributing news that was coming in from all parts of the country about the events of the Putsch, in spite of the fact that the Putsch leaders had ordered these agencies to be closed immediately. I proposed to my colleague from POSTFACTUM that we work together. He agreed and from the morning of August 20, 1991, our publishing house became actively involved in the preparation, printing and distribution of news which was coming f rom all over, little by little. We made photocopies of these news bulletins which we distributed on the streets, in the Metro and at the Russian Parliament, or the White House as it became known. We also started collecting and compiling and cataloguing systematically all the news that was coming into Moscow. As we had this capacity and ability, it w as not difficult for us to collect all the information that was being transmitted by all the media and distributed. This, of course, became the basis of the book PUTSCH.

Very quickly, we started a kind of shuttle service between the Russian Parliament, the center of the opposition to the Putsch, and our publishing house. We started meeting with journalists wherever we could in order to collect information. All the democratic newspapers were banned the first day of the coup d'etat. No newspapers could be published legally. But astonishingly enough, in spite of the events, on the evening of August 19th, the very first day of the coup, the first issue of the newspaper *Moscow News* was actually published secretly. i knew the man who was the editor-in-chief of the *Moscow News*, the organizer and founder of this joint publication, published secretly. I also participated in the *Moscow News* publication and I proposed to my friend that we should work together. He appreciated this very much. We started receiving at our offices at Progress, on our FAX machines, other clandestine or secret newspapers. We made copies of these newspapers on our photocopiers and we distributed them.

We spent a lot of time in this shuttle service between our publishing house and the White House. We not only carried news, but we also carried food. Our kitchen and cafeteria at Progress prepared food for the people who were defending the White House outside and also for those who were defending the White House inside. During those days we hardly had any time to rest.


Q:      Was Progress Publishers closed down by the authorities during the Putsch?


No, not formally. However, on the morning of August 20, 1991, I called a meeting of the staff of Progress. We decided that we would organize a most stringent kind of procedure and regime, much different from normal times. We stepped up security and we did not allow anybody who was not a member of our staff to enter our building. We had our own staff guard our building and we had our younger staff block all t he entrances to our building. Also, you should know that there were five or six military vehicles directly opposite our building with their cannons pointing our way. This was not necessarily designed to intimidate us, but rather to protect the Press Center of the ministry of Foreign Affairs which occupies the building directly opposite ours. Of course, seeing these military vehicles with cannons created a very sinister atmosphere. As well, from the outset of the coup on August 19th, we always heard and recognized the noises of these military vehicles opposite our publishing house and watching them do their military manoeuvres on the concrete and pavement most of whom did not know what was taking place, or why because there did not seem to be any military reason for these vehicles to be there, at all ... all of this really did create a very, very peculiar and unnerving situation for all of us.

Q:  Were you or your friends frightened during these days?

One has to be honest. Of course I was somewhat frightened. I remember early morning of August 19th. I turned on my radio and I heard a very severe voice announce that Mr. Gorbachev was dead and that he could not carry on the functions of the head of state. I was frightened. I immediately thought of my family and my children who were not with me. They were some distance away and I thought of how I could join them and how I could protect them and make them safe. But two hours after that, when I saw the Army enter and occupy the streets of Moscow, this initial fear disappeared. It was replaced by a sense of resistance and defiance. Instead of fear, we decided that we would not allow these people to remain there, to tell us what to do, to direct our lives. We did not want these dictators to remain there, in power. Fear was there for an hour or two. But it was more a kind of confusion of the spirit, a sense of disorientation. We did not know what would happen. Would we be dead, or injured? We did not know, we were somewhat lost at first.

However, what is very important too know is that something strange happened the morning of the Putsch. In our publishing house, many of our editors work at home on their manuscripts. However, the morning of the Putsch, everybody showed u p at work, in their offices. I had the feeling that morning that everybody felt more comfortable and secure being together. Furthermore, everybody was ready to do anything, to work until midnight, if needed, to remain at work, in our publishing house. And during the three nights of the Putsch, many people remained all night long in our publishing house, to protect and guard it, to serve at the coordinating center for information. Everybody was telephoning here all the time wanting to know what was happening in the different parts of the city and in the different regions of the country. There was a genuine sense of fraternity here at that time. It was very moving and truly astonishing.

Q:     How did you organize your information center?

Every two hours we prepared a news bulletin here, in the publishing house. We compiled these bulletins based upon the information that we were assembling here. We made copies of these bulletins and we distributed them from here into the Metros. Everybody was hungry for news. It was quite dangerous on the streets but we still posted these bulletins on the streets and in the Metros. We also prepared a summary of all the news from the clandestine press which we distributed at the White house regularly. Sometimes we were in direct contact with the radio. A small radio station was actually organized and was being transmitted from the offices of the clandestine *Moscow News* newspaper.

On August 20th, when we formally made the decision at Progress to oppose the Putsch and work actively against it, we made this announcement on the radio and that news was rebroadcast on *Radio Moscow*.

Those days were full of astonishing events and activities. Each hour was filled up with telephone calls, news and information which was coming in a little bit from everywhere. People had to be organized so that they could prepare and process the news and information. We really had the feeling then that we were living three years, or three months, but certainly not three days.

Q:     How did those three days affect or change people?

I have the impression that the spirit and souls of people c hanged dramatically and fundamentally because of those events and days. Prior to those days, life was relatively tranquil and normal. But when we saw the Army on our streets, our sense of personal liberty and freedom was menaced. People somehow found a new sense of solidarity, a powerful breath of freedom which fundamentally would not allow the 'putschists' any hope of winning in the struggle. The most astonishing thing was the sense of courage, this profound courage of the people who surrounded the White House during those days to protect it.

It was also a sense of good luck. I remember on August 21st it was announced that the 'putschists' had fled by airplane. Moscow was very dull, it had rained for days, there was a fog. But that day, just after the good news, the sun burst through. It was kind of a symbol.

Three days after the failed Putsch, we all felt like it was the end of the Second World War. Everybody felt like everybody else's brother. There were no superiors or inferiors, everybody was a brother, like soldiers coming out of a war, the whole world was singing, laughing, it was a real holiday, a joy. Unfortunately, it did not last long. Ten days afterwards, life returned to normal and we found ourselves caught up, again, in our problems.

Q:     When did your book actually appear and what was the reaction of people?

The Putsch ended on August 21st. We had our book out on September 10th, 1991. We published 50,000 copies. It was and is very difficult to get a book printed that quickly in Russia. As you can see, we printed on a variety of papers. But we did get the book our in record time.

We launched the book at the opening of the Congress of Deputies of the Russian Republic on September 10th. Everybody was absolutely amazed and surprised when we showed up and started selling the book in the corridors of the Congress and in our Progress bookstore. In two or three days, the entire edition of 50,000 copies was sold out, it simply was gone. We also shipped copies of the book everywhere into the other republics, Siberia, central Asia.

The reality is that the Putsch was most dramatically experienced and felt by the people of Moscow and Leningrad. People who live far from these cities really didn't understand or sense the Putsch. But even in Moscow the reality of the Putsch was experienced most powerfully by a relatively small part of the population.

I remember the morning of the Putsch going by car to my office and seeing people going about their business as if nothing had happened. It is very, very important to remember that the real resistance to the Putsch was led by the young people. They were the ones who went out into the streets, to stop the convoys of military vehicles, who risked their lives at the White house. It is vital to remember this because in our society, we always have the tendency to say that the younger generation is not like the older generation, not nearly as good. One cannot under-estimate the role of the young people in the events of August 19th-21st, 1991.

Our book PUTSCH is not the only record of the events of August 19th-21st. As you know, our publishing house has also organized a video company. For the three days of the Putsch, we had our own cameramen out in the streets of Moscow and in the White House making a video record of the events. These ten hours of tape are the real documentation and documentary of images of the Putsch captured without nostalgia or interpretation. We released a one hour documentary film of the Putsch a few days after the end of the Putsch. The book PUTSCH is very important in our society. As you know, in the past, our history has been Party history and form one generation to the next, in our schools and universities, the image of our history has been changed continuously by the Party to suit itself. Our parents, for example, were taught that during the October 1917 revolution, Stalin stood side-by-side with Lenin and they learned that Stalin was the leader of the revolution, the friend and loyal comrade of Lenin. Our public conscience, our social consciousness is prone to mythology and towards mythologizing the past.

When we decided to prepare this book, what we really wanted to do was to document history, directly, precisely, to become the witnesses to the events of August 1991. Without that true record of these events, in three years from now, or five years, who knows what peculiar gentleman may come along and claim that he was the real 'leader' of the August revolution. At least now, with the publication of the PUTSCH book, in the libraries of Russia, other republics and in other countries, there does exist an accurate and true witness to the events of the Putsch.

*Moscow, December 14, 1991.*

# A NECESSARY FOREWORD

This book is a complete collection of all the information issued by the Russian Information Agency (RIA) from August 19 to 21, 1991. As for the majority of the country's citizens, the attempted state coup was totally unexpected for us RIA journalists, our colleagues and partners in various parts of Russia and the other republics.

Our reporters, correspondents and free-lancers found themselves immediately in the thick of events at the Russian parliament building (the White House), at the barricades, in the regions that supported the State Committee for the State of Emergency and wherever resolute resistance was put up to the anticonstitutional putsch. Now we would like to present for your judgement the information we were able to bring, along all accessible channels, to our audience in Russia, the other republics of the USSR and other countries.

Preparing this manuscript for publication, we decided not to introduce any amendments into the information that came off the teletypes and faxes of the RIA during the days in question. There are, therefore, some announcements that subsequently proved to have been incorrect. This, too, is characteristic of a situation when it is impossible to check the facts as we normally do. For this reason, we wish to apologize profoundly to the reader for the unintentional reflection in some of the material of the emotional tension at the time, of a sharpened perception of events. But we would not wish to change anything at all in this CHRONICLE OF TROUBLED DAYS.

*Andrei Vinogradov,*
*President of the Russian Information Agency*
*August 30, 1991*

# THREE DAYS AT POSTFACTUM

It is not easy to write about revolutionary times: one is already living in a new time, aware of how much more important and risky it is than the past clashes at the turning point--yet it is the actual moment of change that stays in one's memory and, having been dubbed a revolution, casts a dense mythological shadow into the future.

By the morning of August 19, 1991, the situation was such that providing and receiving information about events had become a problem--and not only a technical, but also a personal one--for anyone professionally involved in the mass media: a problem of resistance.

While trying not to appear pretentious, I must insist that for us at the Postfactum agency, August 19 was an ordinary working day. Each one of us realized that an Event had occurred, but events were our livelihood. And, since none of us had been arrested that morning (gift number 1) and the agency had not been closed down (gift number 2) and the telephones were working (a priceless gift!), we simply went about our work. The announcement became fact. Anyone who informed anyone else about what had happened was himself influencing the situation and, moreover, clearly on one side or the other. We, too, interfered. We should like to believe that we did so in a professional manner.

At the same time, while running backwards and forwards between the tanks and barricades, and the faxes, we were fulfilling another special task--we tried not to let our own position influence the essence of what we were announcing. One needs to understand the situation that had then taken shape, with the people who had seized power while themselves knowing little about the country they had decided to capture, not allow anyone to testify, argue or explain anything. While the question of who was to come out on top was being decided, there was no time to consider what was really happening.

Only on the fourth day was there time to do so. Having had no sleep for the Three Days, we devoted the fourth to analyzing what had happened--as far as was possible so close up and tired as we were. This must also have reflected on the articles the reader will find in the analytical section of the book (the first versions of the majority of them were published by Postfactum in the analytical State of Our Country, No. 9, August 23, 1991, which was prepared together with the Centre for Political and Legal Research, INTER-LEGAL).

On the fifth day, the journalist's main festival--the Event--came to an end and that which had been choice became dissolved in everyday work.

*  *  *

I cannot list all those who, during these three days, were with us or came to us to offer help. Yet there can be no doubt that, apart from the authors of the material included here, the following people were among them: Muscovites Alexei Alexeyev, Natalia Arakelova, Anton Arakelov, Tatiana Astakhova, Alexander Avelichev, Anatoli Belyaev, Irina Boyeva, Galina Gornaya, Gleb Grachev, Yelena Fedotova, Filipp Ilyin, Irina Khachaturyan, Larisa Klyuchkovskaya, Vladimir Komissarov, Alexandra Korneyeva, Anna Kovalyova, Galina Kozlova, Alexei Kucherenko, Veronika Kutsyllo, Anna Lebedeva, Oksana Lenda, Raisa Lysenko, Mikhail Lukin, Andrei Makarov, Natalia Malosolova, Ilya Medkov, Ilya Molostvov, Anna Orlova, Inessa Pchelinova, Yelena Perova, Arseni Roginsky, Airat Sakayev, Oleg Semyonov, Andrei Shilov, Yaroslav Skvortsov, Galina Smolina, Valeri Snegovsky, Tatiana Snopkova, Oleg Solodukhin, Kirill Tanayev, Tatiana Trofimova, Elina Vertinskaya, Tatiana Yepifanova, Yevgenia Yesyunina; the agency's correspondents in other cities: Yevgeni Bagayev (Kemerovo), Lyudmila Beletskaya (Kiev), Vladimir Bogodelov (Tyumen), Alexander Bolvachev (Minsk), Eduard Chernov (Sverdlovsk), Vladimir Chukomin (Khanty-Mansiisk), Vladimir Dobrynin (Omsk), Vladislav Dorofeyev (Khabarovsk), Guzel Faizulina (Kazan), Nadezhda Guttenlokher (Novosibirsk), Igor Ivakhnenko (Ashkhabad), Roman Kallas (Tallinn), Gulchachak Khannanova (Ufa), Yevgeni Khlybov (Syktyvkar), Timur Kyuchev (Dushanbe), Yevgeni Kolezyev (Sverdlovsk), Vladimir Korkodym (Kiev), Yelena Kotelnikova (Sverdlovsk), Andrei Kudino (Novosibirsk), Nikolai Kvizhinadze (Tbilisi), Alexei Luzhbin (Perm), Pyotr Martsev (Minsk), Marina Medvedeva (Kazan), Alexei Mikhailik (Magadan), Vladislav Polovtsev (Vorkuta), Andrei Rakul (Rostov-on-Don), Elena Romanenko (Makeevka), Roman Samarin (Daugavpils), Yelena Savicheva (Alma-Ata), Alexander Sukhanov (Tallinn), Victor Titov (Novosibirsk), Ain Toots (Tallinn), Yaroslav Tremblyuk (Kemerovo), Roman Yakovlevsky (Minsk), Alexander Yegorov (Sverdlovsk), Sergei Yerushin (Barnaul),

Anatoli Zakharov (Tomsk), Natalia Zhukova (Leningrad), Victor Zubanyuk (Kiev), and many others. They must all be counted as active participants in the Three Days.

Today, when politics dominate in people's minds and in reports, I should like to remind readers of the role played by non-political organizations during the Three Days. (Were the multitude of anaemic "parties" that existed in the country by August 1991 really of any significance at that time?)

Independent research centres, civil associations, and charitable foundations suddenly united into a reliable network of channels for the transmission of the information, help, and resources necessary for resisting the tanks.

Among these civilian units, I must mention those closest to us: the editors of the journal XX Century and the World and the weekly Kommersant, the Centre for Political and Legal Research and, of course, the Memorial Society, the Institute for Humanitarian and Political Research and, of course, Progress Publishers. The true role and scope were then revealed of the multi-year programme of the Soviet-American Cultural Initiative Fund (known to most people as the Soros Fund), especially the Civil Society programme--groups supported by this programme were active participants in the resistance put up during the Three Days.

The days of resistance united us in common efforts, the result of which--freedom--becomes more and more indistinct with each passing day. Freedom is a state similar to information: it is open, doubtful and dangerous. But it was this risk we wanted.

*Gleb Pavlovsky*
*Director of the Postfactum Information Agency*
*August 30, 1991*

# STATEMENT BY THE SOVIET LEADERSHIP

In connection with the impossibility, owing to his state of health, of Mikhail Sergeevich Gorbachev fulfilling his duties as President of the USSR and with the transfer, according to Article 1277 of the Constitution of the USSR, of the powers of President of the Union of Soviet Socialist Republics to the Vice-President of the USSR Gennadi Yanayev;

for the purpose of overcoming the profound and all-round crisis of political, ethnic and civil confrontation, chaos and anarchy that are threatening the lives and safety of the citizens of the Soviet Union, the sovereignty, territorial integrity, freedom and independence of our Homeland; proceeding from the results of the national referendum on retention of the Union of Soviet Socialist Republics;

governed by the vitally important interests of the peoples of our Homeland, of all Soviet people,

WE DECLARE THAT:

1. In accordance with Article 1273 of the Constitution of the USSR and Article 2 of the Law of the USSR On the Legal Regime of State of Emergency and meeting the demands of broad strata of the population for the adoption of the most decisive measures to prevent a decline of society towards an allover national catastrophe, to ensure law and order, a state of emergency shall be introduced in individual localities of the USSR for a period of six months as of 4.00 a.m. Moscow time, August 19, 1991.

2. The Constitution of the USSR and the laws of the Union of Soviet Socialist Republics shall have unconditional supremacy throughout the territory of the USSR.

3. To govern the country and effectively implement the state of emergency regime, a State Committee for the State of Emergency in the USSR shall be set up, consisting of the following persons: O.D. Baklanov--first deputy chairman of the USSR Defence Council, V.A. Kryuchkov--

chairman of the KGB of the USSR, V.S. Pavlov--Prime Minister of the USSR, B.K. Pugo--Interior Minister of the USSR, V.A. Starodubtsev--chairman of the USSR Peasants Union, A.I. Tizyakov--president of the USSR Association of State Enterprises and Industrial Construction, Transport and Communications Facilities, D.T. Yazov--Defence Minister of the USSR, G.I. Yanayev--acting President of the USSR.

4. The decisions of the Emergency Committee shall be obligatory for unconditional implementation by all organs of power and government, officials and citizens throughout the USSR territory.

*G. Yanayev, V. Pavlov, O. Baklanov*
*August 18, 1991*

RESOLUTION No. 1

State Committee for the State of Emergency in the USSR

For the purpose of defending the vitally important interests of the peoples and citizens of the Union of Soviet Socialist Republics, the independence and territorial integrity of the country, restoring rule of law and order, stabilizing the situation, overcoming the extreme crisis, preventing chaos, anarchy and a fratricidal civil war, the State Committee for the State of Emergency in the USSR resolves that:

1. All organs of power and government of the USSR, the Union and autonomous republics, territories, regions, cities, districts, settlements and villages shall ensure the unconditional compliance with the state of emergency regime in accordance with the Law of the USSR On Legal Regime of State of Emergency and the resolutions of the Emergency Committee. In the event of the inability to ensure the fulfilment of this regime, the powers of the corresponding organs of power and government shall be withdrawn and performance of their functions entrusted to people specially authorized by the Emergency Committee.

2. The structures of power and government, militarized formations acting in contravention to the Constitution of the USSR and the laws of the USSR shall be immediately dissolved.

3. Laws and decisions of organs of power and government contravening the Constitution of the USSR and the laws of the USSR shall henceforth be considered invalid.

4. The activities of political parties, social organizations and mass movements hampering a normalization of the situation shall be halted.

5. In connection with the fact that the State Committee for the State of Emergency in the USSR is temporarily assuming the functions of the Defence Council of the USSR, the activities of the latter shall be halted.

6. Citizens, establishments and organizations shall immediately hand in all illegally possessed types of firearm, ammunition, explosives, military materiel and shells. The Interior Ministry, the KGB and the Ministry of Defence of the USSR shall ensure strict compliance with the given demand. In the event of refusal, they shall take them by force and make violators strictly responsible under both criminal and administrative law.

7. The Procurator's Office, the Interior Ministry, the KGB and the Ministry of Defence of the USSR shall organize effective interaction between the law-enforcing agencies and Armed Forces in ensuring protection of law and order and security of the state, society and citizens in accordance with the Law of the USSR On Legal Regime of State of Emergency and the resolutions of the Emergency Committee.

The holding of meetings, street manifestations, demonstrations, and also strikes shall be prohibited.

When necessary, a curfew, patrolling of the territory and inspections shall be introduced, and measures taken to strengthen the border and customs regimes.

The most important state and economic facilities, as well as the system of essential supplies, shall be taken under control and, in the necessary cases, protection.

A resolute end shall be put to the spread of instigating rumours, actions provoking violations of law and order and inflaming dissension among nationalities, disobedience towards officials engaged in ensuring compliance with the regime of the state of emergency.

8. Control shall be established over the mass media, for which a specially created organ of the Emergency Committee shall be responsible.

9. Organs of power and government and the heads of establishments and enterprises shall take measures to increase the level of organization, establish law and order and discipline in all spheres of the life of society. The normal functioning shall be ensured of enterprises of all branches of the national economy, strict fulfilment of measures to retain and restore, during the period of stabilization, the vertical and horizontal links between economic subjects throughout the USSR territory, the unconditional fulfilment of the established volumes of production, deliveries of raw and other materials and components.

A regime of strict economies of material and technical resources and foreign currency shall be established and maintained, and specific measures shall be implemented to overcome disorganization ans waste of the national wealth.

A resolute struggle shall be waged against the shadow economy and irreversible measures of criminal and administrative responsibility applied to acts of corruption, theft, speculation, concealment of commodities, waste and other violations of law in the sphere of the economy.

Favourable conditions shall be created for increasing the real contribution made by all types of entrepreneurial activity, carried on in accordance with the laws of the Union of Soviet Socialist Republics, to the country's economic potential and the provision of the population with essentials.

10. Work on a permanent basis within the structures of power and government shall be considered incompatible with entrepreneurial activity.

11. Within a week, the Cabinet of Ministers of the USSR shall carry out an inventory of all the available resources of foodstuffs and essentials, inform the people of what the country has at its disposal, and introduce the strictest control over their integrity and distribution.

Any restrictions hampering the movement of foodstuffs and consumer goods, as well as the material resources for their production over the territory of the USSR shall be removed and the observance of this procedure shall be strictly controlled.

Special attention shall be paid to the priority supply of preschool childcare establishments, children's homes, schools, secondary specialized and higher educational institutions, hospitals, as well as pensioners and invalids.

Within a period of one week, proposals shall be made for organizing, freezing and reducing prices of individual types of essentials and foodstuffs, especially for children, the services and public catering, as well as for raising wages and salaries, pensions, allowances, and compensatory payments to various categories of citizen.

Within a period of two weeks, measures shall be elaborated for bringing order to the wage brackets for the heads of state, social, cooperative and other establishments, organizations and enterprises at all levels.

12. Considering the critical situation in harvesting crops and the threat of hunger, extraordinary measures shall be taken to organize the supply, storage and processing of agricultural produce. Working people in the countryside shall be provided with all possible assistance in the form of technology, spare parts, fuel and lubricants and so on. The necessary numbers of blue and white collar workers of enterprises and organizations. students and servicemen shall be sent to the countryside immediately to save the harvest.

13. Within a period of one week, the Cabinet of Ministers of the USSR shall elaborate a resolution envisaging the provision in 1991-92 of all townspeople who wish with allotments of 0.15 hectares for growing fruit and vegetables.

14. Within a period of two weeks, the USSR Cabinet of Ministers shall complete the planning of urgent measures to bring the country's fuel and energy complex out of crisis and prepare for the winter.

15. Within a period of one month prepare and inform the people of measures for 1992 for a fundamental improvement in housing construction and provision of the population with housing.

In the course of six months, a specific programme shall be elaborated for the accelerated development of state, co-operative and individual housing construction for a five-year period.

16. The central and local organs of power and government shall devote priority attention to the social needs of the population. Possibilities shall be sought for substantially improving free medical services and public education.

RESOLUTION No. 2
The State Committee for the State of Emergency in the USSR
ON THE PUBLICATION OF CENTRAL, MOSCOW CITY AND REGIONAL NEWSPAPERS

In connection with the introduction on August 19, 1991 in Moscow and certain other territories of the Union of Soviet Socialist Republics of the state of emergency and in accordance with Point 14, Article 4, of the Law of the USSR On Legal Regime of State of Emergency, the State Committee for the State of Emergency in the USSR resolves:

1. Temporarily to limit the number of central, Moscow city and regional socio-political publications to the following newspapers: Trud, Rabochaya tribuna, Izvestia, Pravda, Krasnaya zvezda, Sovetskaya Rossiya, Moskovskaya pravda, Leninskoye znamya and Selskaya zhizn.

2. The renewal of publication of other central, Moscow city and regional newspapers and socio-political publications shall be decided by a specially created organ of the Emergency Committee.

*State Committee for the State of Emergency in the USSR*
*August 19, 1991*

## DECREE

of the Acting President of the Union of Soviet Socialist Republics
ON THE INTRODUCTION OF THE STATE OF EMERGENCY IN
THE CITY OF MOSCOW

In connection with the exacerbation of the situation in the city of Moscow--the capital of the Union of Soviet Socialist Republics--engendered by non-fulfilment of Resolution No. 1 of the State Committee for the State of Emergency in the USSR of August 19, 1991, attempts to organize meetings, street demonstrations and manifestations, incidents of instigation to disorderly conduct, in the interests of protection and security of citizens, in accordance with Article 1273 of the Constitution of the USSR, I resolve:

1. To declare a state of emergency in the city of Moscow as of August 19, 1991.

2. To appoint, as commandant of the city of Moscow, the commander of the troops of the Moscow military district, Lt. Gen. N.V.Kalinin, who is empowered to issue obligatory orders regulating issues of maintaining the state of emergency regime.

*G. Yanayev*
*Acting President of the USSR*
*Moscow, the Kremlin, August 19, 1991*
*(Pravda, January 20, 1991)*

# THE DIARY

AUGUST 19TH, 1991

4.00 (PF). The Sevastopol regiment of the USSR KGB forces blockaded M.S. Gorbachev's dacha at Foros in the Crimea. The runway at Belbek, where the President's flight--a TU-134 plane and an MI-8 helicopter--were located, was blocked by two trucks. This was done on the orders of one of the plotters--Maj. Gen. Maltsev, the head of the country's air defence forces.

4.30 (PF). In Moscow, someone authorized by one of the members of the Emergency Committee rang a Russian TV head official at home and warned him of the impending coup.

6.00 (PF). The USSR Minister of Defence D. Yazov held a meeting of the commanders of the military districts. The instruction came down to the following: to ensure law and order depending on the situation--strengthen the protection of military facilities. "You will learn about the rest from radio and newspaper announcements," the Minister said.

VILNIUS. At 8.25 a.m., units of the Soviet Army seized the building of the Kaunas radio and television centre. The radio and TV broadcasts were halted, but the Lithuanian radio in Vilnius continued broadcasting (Smena, St. Petersburg, Aug. 20).

09.12 Moscow time. THE FAR EAST: SITUATION NORMAL

VLADIVOSTOK (RIA). At 9.00 Moscow time, the situation in Vladivostok was normal. There were no military on the streets.

09.20. LITHUANIA: PARATROOPS HAVE OCCUPIED THE TV AND RADIO CENTRE IN KAUNAS

VILNIUS (RIA). In Vilnius, on the morning of Aug. 19, the situation was normal, with no more military on the streets than usual.

At 9.00 the Chairman of the Supreme Soviet of the Republic, Vitautas Landsbergis, addressed the citizens of Lithuania. He announced that the first possible victim in the Baltics would be the TV and radio centre in Kaunas, which troops had been unable to take on January 13. Troop movements had been observed near the TV centre. Landsbergis proposed urgently calling the parliament of the Republic.

As the Elta agency reported, referring to the Lithuanian government press bureau, this morning between 8.25 and 9.00, paratroopers occupied all local radio and TV facilities in Kaunas.

### 9.40. MOSCOW: THE SITUATION IS NOT CLEAR YET

MOSCOW (RIA). From 9.30 on Aug. 19, individual military columns--army lorries, APCs and tanks, began movement. USSR President Mikhail Gorbachev's press service announced that they were working as usual. No military activity is observed in or around the Kremlin. Only on individual main roads there are military traffic controllers. As an RIA corespondent found out, the Russian TV building is blockaded and it will not be broadcasting.

### 10.00. INFORMATION FROM THE PRESS SERVICE OF THE RUSSIAN MINISTRY OF FOREIGN AFFAIRS

MOSCOW (RIA). All foreign correspondents are invited today at 11.00 a.m. to receive information concerning today's events. Entry will be through entrance No. 1a of the Russian parliament building by accreditation card. The press conference will probably be held by Boris Yeltsin.

### 11.20. LENINGRAD: SPEECH BY THE CITY MILITARY COMMANDANT

PSKOV (RIA). The military commandant of Leningrad spoke on local radio. He called for all weapons to be withdrawn from the population, for duplicators, copy machines, and the mass media to be brought under control. A salvation committee has been formed, including the First Secretary of the Leningrad regional committee of the CPSU, Boris Gidaspov.

### 11.30. ANNOUNCEMENT BY THE RUSSIAN PRESIDENT'S INFORMATION DEPARTMENT

MOSCOW (RIA). "The announcements spread by certain people that Boris Yeltsin is calling on the people to gather at 12.00 on Manege Square are pure provocation," said Valentin Sergeyev, head of the Russian President's information department, to an RIA correspondent.

## 11.34. TO THE CITIZENS OF RUSSIA

MOSCOW (RIA). We are passing on the Appeal to the citizens of Russia:

"On the night of August 18 to 19, 1991 the country's legally elected President was removed from power.

"Whatever the reasons given to justify this, we are dealing with a right-wing reactionary, anticonstitutional coup.

"For all the difficulties and serious trials suffered by the people, the democratic process in the country is acquiring increasing depth and an irreversible character. The peoples of Russia are becoming the masters of their own fate. The arbitrary powers of non-constitutional organs, including Party ones, have been substantially curtailed. The leadership of Russia has taken a resolute stand concerning the Union Treaty, striving for integrity of the Soviet Union and of Russia. Our position on this issue has made it possible to speed up substantially the preparations for this Treaty, to come to an agreement on it with all the republics and determine the date for its signing--August 20 of this year.

"This development of events gave rise to animosity on the part of the reactionary forces, prompting them to make irresponsible adventuristic attempts to resolve the extremely complex political and economic problems by means of force. Attempts at a coup had already been made.

"We believed and still believe that such forcible means are unacceptable. They discredit the USSR in the eyes of the whole world, undermine our prestige in the world community, caste us back to the era of the cold war and isolation of the Soviet Union from the world community.

"All this compels us to declare the so-called committee that has come to power unlawful. Correspondingly, we declare all the decisions and resolutions of this committee invalid.

"We are convinced that the local government bodies will unconditionally comply with the constitutional laws and Decrees of the President of Russia.

"We call on all citizens of Russia to make a worthy response to the leaders of the putsch and demand that the country be returned to its normal constitutional development.

"It is, of course, necessary to ensure the possibility of the country's President, Gorbachev, speaking to the nation. We demand the immediate convocation of an Extraordinary Congress of People's Deputies of the USSR.

"We are absolutely sure that our countrymen will not permit the arbitrary power and lawlessness of the shameless and conscienceless leaders of the putsch. We call on members of the armed forces to demonstrate a high level of civil duty and not participate in the reactionary coup.

"Until these demands are fulfilled, we call for a general indefinite strike.

"We do not doubt that the world community will give an objective assessment to the cynical attempt at a right-wing coup.

*RSFSR President B.N. Yeltsin*
*Chairman of the RSFSR Council of Ministers I.S. Silayev*
*Acting Chairman of the RSFSR Supreme Soviet R.I. Khasbulatov*
*August 19, 1991, 9.00 a.m."*

## 11.00. STATE OF EMERGENCY, LENINGRAD

LENINGRAD (RIA). At 10.00 a.m. the Commandant of Leningrad, Col. Gen. Victor Samsonov, spoke on Leningrad radio and television. He announced that a committee had been formed for the state of emergency, including: Victor Samsonov--commander of the Leningrad military district and military commandant of Leningrad, Vyacheslav Shcherbakov--first deputy mayor of Leningrad, chairman of the commission for emergency situations, Yarov--chairman of the Leningrad Regional Soviet, Anatoli Kurkov--chairman of the Leningrad KGB department, Victor Khramtsov--deputy chairman of the commission for emergency situations.

A special procedure is being introduced in Leningrad for the appointment and movement of heads of enterprises. Dismissal of workers at their own wish, strikes, meetings, and trade in alcoholic beverages are prohibited. Restrictions are also being introduced on the use of video and audio equipment and various duplicating machines. Control is being established over the mass media. Restrictions are being introduced on the movement of means of transport and a special regime for the use of all means of communication.

According to an RIA corespondent, on Aug. 20 a plenary session of the Leningrad regional committee of the CPSU was planned. It is assumed that it was to remove Boris Gidaspov.

## 11.49. STATE OF EMERGENCY, RYAZAN

RYAZAN (RIA). According to data received by the RIA, a state of emergency has been introduced in Ryazan. It has been announced that local deputies have been deprived of their deputy immunity. Meetings have been prohibited in the town. Control over the mass media has been introduced.

## 11.54. STATE OF EMERGENCY, MOSCOW: IF SERVICEMEN RECEIVE AN ORDER, IT WILL BE CARRIED OUT

MOSCOW (RIA). There are ten APCs with paratroopers around the TASS building. A captain refused to tell an RIA correspondent what military task had been set for his unit. Without giving his name, he commented thus on the events: "The army is not respected." In answer to the correspondent's question as to whether his unit would use arms against the population, the captain said: "If such an order is given, what can we do?" It is thought that the column might move in the direction of Pushkin Square and block the city's main thoroughfare.

12.00. CONGRESS OF EXPATRIATES PROCEEDS NORMALLY

MOSCOW (RIA). "We are doing our best not to involve our guests in the political struggle," said the chairman of the organizing committee of the Congress of Expatriates, Mikhail Tolstoy, to an RIA correspondent in connection with the latest events in the country. Tolstoy stated that, at the given moment, there had been no changes in the programme of the congress, which had opened on August 19, although there would be changes in the process of the work of the forum. Tolstoy also remarked that the telephone links between the Rossiya Hotel, where the guests were staying and the congress headquarters were located, and the Russian Supreme Soviet, had not been broken off. Evidently, President of Russia Boris Yeltsin would not be speaking at the official opening of the Congress, planned for 7.00 p.m. on August 19. The situation behind the scenes at the congress was calm. The participants in the congress had made no statements concerning the latest events.

SYKTYVKAR (PF). At 12.00 was held an expanded session of the Coordinating Council of the Syktyvkar branch of the Democratic Russia. At the session the decision was adopted to launch a campaign of civil disobedience against the State Emergency Committee, which has seized power in the USSR. The presidium of the Komi Autonomous Republic Supreme Soviet, which met before lunch, decided not to make any appeals to the citizens of the Komi Republic before the return of Komi Supreme Soviet Chairman Yuri Spiridonov and Council of Ministers Chairman Vyacheslav Khudyaev, who were in Moscow for the signing of the Union Treaty. In the capital of the Komi Republic the situation is calm. No statements have yet been received by the mass media from the Interior Ministry, the KGB or military garrison.

12.13. STATE OF EMERGENCY, MOSCOW: STATEMENT BY PRESI-DENT OF RUSSIA AT PRESS CONFERENCE

MOSCOW (RIA). President of the Russian Federation Boris Yeltsin called recent events in the USSR a rightist coup. Speaking today at a press conference at the Russian parliament building, he told journalists that the leaders of the Ukraine and several other republics with whom he had had an opportunity to speak share this view of events. According to Yeltsin, he has not yet been able to contact President of the USSR Mikhail Gorbachev. He remarked that radio and television have been placed under special control by the putschists. Commenting on Resolution No. 1 of the Emergency

Committee, he said that he sees it as proof of a coup and said that the leadership of the Russian Federation would continue to firmly carry out its duties, underlining that the Russian President received his powers from the people and that no one has a right to remove him. Yeltsin reported that a decree of the President of Russia would be issued today on the disobedience to the orders of the illegal committee on the territory of the Russian Federation.

## 12.19. STATE OF EMERGENCY, MOSCOW: DEMONSTRATION OUTSIDE THE MOSCOW CITY SOVIET BUILDING

MOSCOW (RIA). A spontaneous demonstration is occurring opposite the Moscow City Soviet building. Ten armoured troop carriers have appeared from the direction of Mayakovsky Square. Crowds have blocked off Tverskaya Street to prevent the movement of the APCs towards the Kremlin. Something resembling tin cans are being hurled into the crowds of people from the APCs. Rumours are being spread among the demonstrators that gas will be used.

According to reports, the Russian parliament building on the Krasnopresnenskaya Embankment has been surrounded by tanks.

## 12.32. STATE OF EMERGENCY, MOSCOW: SITUATION IN THE CENTRE OF THE CITY

MOSCOW (RIA). Armoured troop carriers are moving towards the city's centre. They have been stopped by crowds assembled outside the Moscow City Soviet building. Demonstrators have climbed atop of the APCs holding placards that say, "No to Fascism!" Some are saying that Boris Yeltsin is calling upon everyone to strike and will announce this at the Manege Square.

At 12.30 the APCs turned around and went back carrying with them the demonstrators and placards. A tricolour Russian flag has been hung on a window on the Moscow City Soviet building.

KHABAROVSK (PF). Sergei Markarov, first secretary of the Khabarovsk Territory Committee of the Russian Communist Party told PF: "In the Emergency Committee are strong-willed statesmen who are not indifferent about the fate of Russia. They can be trusted fully, they will introduce order in the country. I am for order and for union laws." Maj. Gen. Vitali Pirozhnyak, head of the Khabarovsk Territory KGB stated: "According to our information, a state of emergency will not be imposed in Khabarovsk Territory. We will work under all circumstances, and unless ordered to do so, will not change our position. But, in my view, the armed units created by the republican government should be treated with respect."

Col. Gen. Victor Novozhilov, commander-in-chief of the Far East Military District, said: "I first heard about the state of emergency over the radio at the same time as everyone else."

Vladimir Butenko, chief of troops of the Far East Border District, said: "We don't care who's in power--Gorbachev or Andropov. We guarded the border and will continue to guard the border. In general we have no time for discussions--the border area is flooded."

Vladimir Balanov, chief of the Interior Department of the Khabarovsk Territory Executive Committee, said: "Our job is to ensure perfect order so that the right-wingers don't fight with the left-wingers."

## 12.36. STATE OF EMERGENCY, MOSCOW: CITY'S COMMANDANT REPORTED THAT ALL IS QUIET IN MOSCOW

MOSCOW (RIA). At the Moscow's commandant office an RIA correspondent was told that "all is quiet in the capital, the situation is being controlled, a state of emergency has not been introduced". They failed to explain the presence of military hardware in the streets, but they did say that force would not be used and by nightfall all vehicles and military units would leave the city.

## 12.44. STATE OF EMERGENCY, MOSCOW: PARLIAMENTARY FACTION SOYUZ SUPPORTS STATEMENT OF STATE COMMITTEE FOR STATE OF EMERGENCY

MOSCOW (RIA). The parliamentary faction Soyuz supports the announcement of the State Emergency Committee, said Georgi Tikhonov, a member of the presidium of this group of federal legislators in a telephone interview with an RIA correspondent. According to Tikhonov, the Soyuz leadership knew nothing of this impending action. Asked about the possibility of the leaders of the Soyuz faction participating in the Committee, Tikhonov said, "We intend to restrict our activity within the USSR Supreme Soviet." Tikhonov, who is a deputy of the USSR Supreme Soviet, also said that he has information that several Union republics support the removal of President USSR Mikhail Gorbachev.

## 12.46. STATE OF EMERGENCY, LITHUANIA: CHIEF OF VILNIUS GARRISON GEN. FROLOV REFUSES TO SAY WHAT KIND OF ACTIONS ARMY WILL TAKE IN LITHUANIA

MOSCOW (RIA). Chief of the Vilnius garrison Valeri Frolov refused to say what his troops might do in Lithuania. "It's my business," he said in a telephone interview with RIA, and added, "Keep tabs on the situation." Meanwhile, according to reports from Vilnius, the situation in the city is calm. The troops have yet to take any actions. Thousands of people have gathered outside the Lithuanian parliament building to protect their legally elected authority after an appeal was issued by Lithuanian leader Vytautas Landsbergis.

12.49. DEMONSTRATION ON MANEGE SQUARE

Moscow (RIA). An RIA correspondent reported that at 11.45 the first group of demonstrators appeared on Manege Square carrying posters that said "Fascism Won't Pass!", "Freedom!" and "Yazov, Pugo and Kryuchkov on Trial!" No attempts have yet been made to disperse the crowd, nor were troops visible. The demonstrators, shouting "Fascist!", drove from the square the leader of the Liberal Democratic Party of the USSR Vladimir Zhirinovsky.

12.50. STATE OF EMERGENCY, ESTONIA: STATEMENT OF EMERGENCY DEFENCE COUNCIL OF ESTONIAN REPUBLIC

TALLINN (RIA). The Emergency Defence Council of the Estonian Republic met on Aug. 19 to discuss the situation in the Soviet Union in connection with the changes in the Soviet leadership announced in the morning of Aug. 19. The meeting was chaired by Arnold Ruutel, chairman of the republic's Supreme Soviet. The Emergency Defence Council of Estonia appealed to all citizens of the Estonian Republic, self-government bodies and state and public organizations to remain calm and keep their spirits up. The democratically elected bodies of power and the government of Estonia in the given situation will continue the course towards the peaceful restoration of Estonia's independence, it was stressed at the meeting.

12.51. APPEAL BY VYTAUTAS LANDSBERGIS TO THE PEOPLES OF THE WORLD AND GOVERNMENTS OF FREE COUNTRIES, TO THE UN AND OTHER INTERNATIONAL ORGANIZATIONS

VILNIUS (RIA). Chairman of the Supreme Soviet of Lithuania Vytautas Landsbergis issued an appeal today over radio to the peoples of the world, the governments of free countries, the UN and other international organizations. In it he stated that people's lives and public order in the Lithuanian Republic were endangered by the risk of Soviet military violence.

"Assist the legally elected Lithuanian government. Proclaim while it is not too late that the introduction of occupational Soviet power in Lithuania will be a continuation of the Hitler-Stalin deal, that Western countries will not tolerate the new Stalinism and that all responsibility for the consequences of aggression will lay with those who initiate and execute this violence," Landsbergis stated. He also said that he had received a telephone call today from the commander-in-chief of the Baltic Military District, Fyodor Kuzmin demanding that employees of Lithuania's Territorial Defence Department be disarmed. Landsbergis said he rejected Kuzmin's demand.

SVERDLOVSK (PF). Deputy Chairman of the Sverdlovsk Regional Soviet Anatoli Grebenkin said in an interview with Postfactum that the "statement of the Soviet leadership" was tantamount to "an attempted military coup". Grebenkin said that after the statement was read over the radio the Sverdlovsk Regional Executive Committee called an emergency meeting. According to Grebenkin, the leaders of the Sverdlovsk Region are now waiting for a reaction to the "Soviet leadership's statement" from the office of Russian President Boris Yeltsin.

## 13.08. STATE OF EMERGENCY, MOSCOW: DEMONSTRATION IN THE CITY'S CENTRE

MOSCOW (RIA). At noon on Moscow's Manege Square an unplanned demonstration was staged by several thousand people with many more joining them as the minutes pass. A statement by the Russian leadership was read out at the meeting calling the events of the night of Aug. 19 an "unconstitutional coup" and appealing for a "general unlimited strike." A column of armoured vehicles began moving towards Manege Square from the direction of the Bolshoi Theatre soon after the start of the demonstration but several thousand people stood in the path of the vehicles, their arms linked together, to prevent the vehicles from entering the square. At 12.30 demonstrators positioned two trolleybuses outside the National Hotel to block off Tverskaya Street. Ten buses carrying special assualt squads have appeared on the scene, along with ambulances. Demonstrators have cordoned off the square. According to unconfirmed reports, Vitali Urazhtsev, a deputy of the Russian parliament and chairman of the union for the defence of servicemen's rights, Shield, was arrested at around ten o'clock this morning outside the Russian parliament building.

Meanwhile, military vehicles continue to move about Moscow. Tanks with unsheathed guns stand at the entrances of all bridges. Traffic on Tverskaya Street has been interrupted by armoured vehicles. The commandant of Moscow Nikolai Smirnov told the Russian Information Agency that a state of emergency has been declared in Moscow and that troops have been stationed in Moscow "to maintain order and prevent terrorist acts". He also said that he knows nothing of the whereabouts of USSR President Mikhail Gorbachev.

13.00 (PF). Boris Yeltsin came out of the Russian parliament building and mounted tank number 110 of the Taman Division from where he called on all citizens of Russia to give a worthy response to the putschists and demand that the country be returned to a normal constitutional development.

13.17. STATE OF EMERGENCY, MOSCOW: TANK COLUMNS
MOSCOW (RIA). According to eyewitness reports, a long column of tanks travelling along Minsk Highway entered Moscow at 12.30, heading towards the centre of Moscow.

13.32. A STATE OF EMERGENCY WILL NOT BE IMPOSED IN KAZAKHSTAN
Alma Ata (RIA). On the evening of Aug. 19 it is expected that President of Kazakhstan Nursultan Nazarbayev will speak to the republic's people. The government is now in session here. RIA has learned that a state of emergency will not be imposed in Kazakhstan. Sunday evening Nazarbayev had a telephone conversation with USSR President Mikhail Gorbachev in a normal and friendly manner.

13.39. STATE OF EMERGENCY, MOSCOW: EMERGENCY SESSION OF RUSSIAN SUPREME SOVIET HAS BEEN SCHEDULED
MOSCOW (RIA). Acting chairman of the Russian Federation Supreme Soviet Ruslan Khasbulatov told a press conference at the Russian parliament building that the Presidium of the RUSSIAN Supreme Soviet met on Aug. 19 and adopted a resolution to convene an emergency session of the Russian Supreme Soviet on Aug. 21, 1991. There will be one item on the agenda: the political situation in the republic as a result of the coup d'etat.

SEVEROURALSK, SVERDLOVSK REGION (PF). Miners of the Sevuralboksitrud production association have gone out on strike. The chairman of the Independent Miners Union committee, Alexander Yefremov, told Postfactum that at 2.00 p.m. local time around 300 miners employed at mines number sixteen and fourteen began a political strike.

BARNAUL (PF). The mass media of the Altai Territory have not broadcast on Aug. 19 the documents signed on this day by the leaders of Russia. Meanwhile representatives of the region's democratic movement have circulated these documents. (Rossiiskaya gazeta, August 23, 1991.)

DZERZHINSK, NIZHNY NOVGOROD REGION (PF). At a meeting of the Presidium of the City Soviet the decision was made to carry out the resolutions and decrees of the Russian government and the President of Russia. The local police are under the control of the City Soviet, as is the city radio station, over which twice over the course of Monday were read the documents of the Russian leadership. (Rossiiskaya gazeta, August 23, 1991.)

ROSTOV-ON-DON (PF). An emergency committee in support of the State Emergency Committee has been created. It has taken control of the local mass media. (Rossiiskaya gazeta, August 23, 1991.)

Taganrog (PF). The presidium of the regional executive committee decided to support the President of Russia. (Rossiiskaya gazeta, August 23, 1991.)

## 13.44. STATE OF EMERGENCY, MOSCOW: DECREE OF THE PRESIDENT OF RUSSIA

MOSCOW (RIA). In connection with the actions of a group of persons calling themselves the State Committee for the State of Emergency, I decree:

1. Regard the committee's statement as anticonstitutional and qualify the actions of its organizers as a coup d'etat, which is none other than a state crime.

2. All decisions made on behalf of the so-called State Emergency Committee should be regarded as illegal and without force on the territory of the Russian Federation. On the territory of the Russian Federation is functioning the legally elected authority in the person of the President, Supreme Soviet and Chairman of the Council of Ministers, and all state and local government bodies of the Russian Federation.

3. Actions of officials carrying out the decisions of the above-named committee come under the effect of the Criminal Code of the Russian Federation and are subject to punishment by law.

This decree comes into effect at the time of its signing.

*President of the Russian Federation Boris Yeltsin*

## 14.00. STATE OF EMERGENCY, MOSCOW: SITUATION AS OF 13.30

MOSCOW (RIA). Several tanks entered Okhotny Ryad at Theatre Square and headed in the direction of Lubyanka. A motorized rifle unit is stationed near the Bolshoi Theatre. The approaches to Manege Square have been blocked off by trolleybuses. Buses carrying special assault troops are parked on the side of the History Museum. A column of armoured vehicles tired to pass between the Manege and Alexander Gardens but were prevented from doing so by demonstrators. According to speakers at a rally here, the Central Telegraph building is under the control of the State Emergency Committee. Major Victor Gogolev, standing atop an APC, told the crowds that there were no orders to shoot and demonstrated the empty cartridge of his gun. Deputy of the Moskvoretsky District Soviet, Vladimir Ivanov, told the rally that the Likhachev Auto Works, the Kalibr, and the axle plant were on strike. He also reported that People's Deputy of the USSR Telman Gdlyan had been arrested. Trucks equipped with water cannons tried to enter the square at 13.20 but were forced to retreat to a place outside the building of the journalism department of Moscow University after demonstrators attacked the vehicles. Many demonstrators began leaving the square for the Krasnopresnenskaya Embankment near the Russian parliament building. On both sides of the bridge across the Moscow River are parked tanks with their guns pointed towards the street. Tanks and armoured vehicles have been seen repeatedly moving along the Garden Ring Road in the vicinity of Zubovskaya Square. A large number of troops and military vehicles have assembled near the Russian parliament building.

## 14.06 SAJUDIS' APPEAL TO RESIDENTS OF LITHUANIA

Vilnius (RIA). The Sajudis Council issued on Aug. 19 an appeal to the residents of Lithuania saying that if Soviet troops succeed in overthrowing the legitimate government a general political strike should be started. It also called on residents of the republic to assembly on the central squares of cities and district centres.

## 14.11. STATE OF EMERGENCY, VLADIVOSTOK: PRIMORYE BRANCH OF DEMOCRATIC RUSSIA URGES GIVING REBUFF TO REACTION

VLADIVOSTOK (RIA). The Primorye branch of the Democratic Russia called the situation that has emerged in the country on Aug. 19 an "illegal military coup." It called on all democratically minded residents of the Primorye Territory to unite their efforts and give a rebuff to the reactionary forces. A rally in Vladivostok has been scheduled for Aug. 20.

## 14.20. LEADER OF LATVIAN COMMUNISTS WELCOMES ACTIONS BY STATE EMERGENCY COMMITTEE

MOSCOW (RIA). Alfred Rubiks, a member of the CPSU Central Committee Politburo and first secretary of the Latvian Communist Party declared at a press conference held Aug. 19 in Riga that he was following today's developments "not only with joy but with sorrow." "This was the dream of our Communist Party," he said. He also said that Latvia was one of the six regions of the country were a six-month state of emergency was being imposed, and that all power was being transferred to an emergency committee to be formed the next day by the commander-in-chief of the Baltic Military District, Fyodor Kuzmin. The Bureau of the Latvian Communist Party's Central Committee and "Equal Rights" faction of the Latvian parliament, representing the interests of the republic's Russian population, would offer their membership on this interim body. All political parties whose activities contradict the Constitution of the USSR and of the Latvian Republic would be banned, and the news media that do not support the new order would be closed.

Rubiks also said that charges would be filed against a number of "extremist" deputies and that units defending the Latvian Supreme Soviet building would be disarmed. He stated that all attempts--especially armed-- to resist the emergency committee would be suicidal.

## 14.37. NINA ANDREYEVA SUPPORTS DECLARATION OF STATE OF EMERGENCY

MOSCOW (RIA). Leader of the nationwide Yedinstvo (Unity) society, Nina Andreyeva, declared on behalf of the society that it fully supported the statement by the so-called State Emergency Committee and its subsequent actions. In her statement, read to RIA over the telephone from Leningrad, Andreyeva said that Unity "anticipated that the State Emergency Committee would take decisive actions to impose socialist order in the country and pull the USSR from its deep crisis". Andreyeva said that she hoped a thorough investigation would be conducted "into the activities of the plotters and organizers of the counter-revolution who have encroached upon the constitutional system." Nina Andreyeva told an RIA correspondent that she thought that a majority of the country's population supported the actions of the State Emergency Committee but that in Moscow and Leningrad "the reaction would be negative, there would be much commotion."

14.43. STATE OF EMERGENCY, LENINGRAD: EMERGENCY SESSION OF LENINGRAD CITY SOVIET CALLED

LENINGRAD (RIA). Chairman of the Leningrad City Soviet, Alexander Belyayev said that an emergency session of the Leningrad City Soviet was scheduled for 4.00 p.m. on Aug. 19. The deputy police chief of Leningrad, Victor Frolov reported that the police were ready for an emergency situation and were being reinforced by people who would not lose their heads in any situation. He said that the police were counting on the public to be supportive and reasonable. The press centre of the local KGB refused to comment on events and said that their knowledge was limited to what they had heard on the radio. However one officer said privately that all this was "nasty". On orders of Vice-Mayor Vyacheslav Scherbakov, who is a member of the emergency committee for ruling Leningrad, OMON squads have been deployed on the outskirts of Leningrad.

The Leningrad branch of the Democratic Russia intends to dispatch delegates to major factories to agitate for a general strike. Representatives of the Kirov Works are reporting to the Leningrad City Soviet that the works is ready to strike. The reception office of Alexander Belyayev, the chairman of the Leningrad City Soviet, reports that the Pskov Airborne Division is heading for Leningrad.

More than 1,000 people have gathered outside the Leningrad City Soviet building. The demonstrators are carrying signs that read, "Everyone on Strike!" and "No to the Fascist Junta!" Several Leningrad City Soviet deputies have joined them.

14.49 STATE OF EMERGENCY: MINERS CONSIDERING POSSIBILITY OF POLITICAL STRIKE

MOSCOW (RIA). In mining centres throughout the country the situation appears to be calm. According to reports from Kemerovo, an expanded session of the Council of Workers' Committees is scheduled to meet in Prokopyevsk at 19.00 local time. The session will discuss the situation in the country and the possible actions of workers. The likelihood of a miners' strike in the Kuznetsk Basin is high.

In Karaganda, where not long ago the strike committee was disbanded, there is news of an imminent strike or other actions.

In the Vorkuta strike committee RIA was told that the actions of the State Emergency Committee would be deemed a coup d'etat until something was heard from the Presidents of the USSR and Russia Mikhail Gorbachev and Boris Yeltsin over the television or radio. A meeting of the strike committee is scheduled for the Aug. 19 at which the decision would be made to take part in a political strike. The strike committee also said that it supports the legally elected leadership of Russia.

VOLGOGRAD (PF). The presidium of the regional Soviet supported the President of Russia. The texts of the Russian President's decrees were read over regional television and radio and were published in the Volgograd evening. The heads of the regional KGB and police reported that they would obey the orders of the Russian government. (Rossiiskaya gazeta, August 23, 1991.)

TOMSK (PF). Chairman of the regional Soviet Victor Kress, chairman of the city Soviet Anatoli Cherkassky, chairman of the city executive committee Vladimir Gonchar and Russian Supreme Soviet member Daniil Dobzhinsky issued appeals to the residents of Tomsk over regional radio. Cherkassky stated that the actions of the new leadership did not correspond to the situation in the country. Gonchar said that the leaders of Tomsk did not support the new course. Dobzhinsky remarked that the developments in the country resembled an attempted military coup.

## 14.57. RUSSIAN RADIO AND TELEVISION STOP BROADCASTING

MOSCOW (RIA). RIA has just learned that on Aug. 19 and 20 Russian television and radio on orders from the State Television Radio Broadcasting Company chairman Leonid Kravchenko, will not go on the air. However their editorial offices continue to work and are prepared at a moment's notice to broadcast information on reaction at home and abroad to the events of Aug. 19. The operating schedule for Aug. 21 is not yet known.

## 15.09. REACTION IN AZERBAIJAN TO TAKEOVER BY STATE EMERGENCY COMMITTEE

BAKU (RIA). Isa Gambarov, a People's Deputy of Azerbaijan and chief of the organization department of the Azerbaijani Popular Front thinks that the changes in the USSR leadership will have less of an effect in Azerbaijan than in other republics, the Turan news agency reports. Gambarov cited the conservative bent of the current local government and the fact that Azerbaijan has been under a state of emergency for more than a year already.

Another member of the Azerbaijani Supreme Soviet, who preferred to remain anonymous, called the change of government in the country a stabilizing factor.

Both believe that the changes in the country could have a positive effect on the resolution of the Armenian-Azerbaijani conflict in Nagorny Karabakh.

OMSK (PF). Vladimir Varnavksy, chairman of the Omsk City Soviet and a deputy to the Russian parliament learned of the creation of the State Emergency Committee and the resignation of Gorbachev from Postfactum. Said Varnavsky: "This appears to be a gesture of desperation--and a setback." Assistant professor at the Omsk Police Academy Yuri Solovey, who helped draft the Russian law on the police, told Postfactum: "All this seems to be an attempt to return to the old, the final chance of the conservatives." In his opinion, this attempt does not appear to be serious and is unlikely to be successful. It has been learned from sources close to the regional KGB that the chief of the local KGB, Maj. Gen. Alexei Bannikov knew nothing about the impending change of leadership.

KHABAROVSK (PF). Chairman of the Khabarovsk Territory Executive Committee Valeri Litvinov refused to comment on the situation, telling Postfactum: "I am constantly on the telephone, I know nothing more than you do and I am waiting to see whether or not a state of emergency will be declared in Khabarovsk." Victor Ishayev, first deputy chairman of the Khabarovsk Territory Executive Committee said, "They should have removed Gorbachev three years ago. Something had to be done." Several programmes have been cancelled on Khabarovsk radio but, according to some reports, no specific instructions have yet been issued. Police vehicles have appeared at all major intersections in Khabarovsk.

## 15.32. STATE OF EMERGENCY, MOSCOW: APPEAL BY RUSSIAN SECRETARY OF STATE

MOSCOW (RIA). Russian Secretary of State Gennadi Burbulis requested that all fax machines on the territory of Russia be left turned on and ready to receive information.

## 15.21. ANATOLIJS GORBUNOVS CALLED ANATOLI LUKYANOV

RIGA (RIA). Chairman of the Supreme Soviet of Latvia Anatolijs Gorbunovs told the Latvian parliament that he had spoken by telephone with Chairman of the USSR Supreme Soviet Anatoli Lukyanov. According to the Leta news agency, Gorbunovs asked Lukyanov whether a state of emergency had been imposed in Latvia, and Lukyanov replied that as far as he knew, no. Lukyanov also said that the USSR Supreme Soviet would be convened to consider the legal aspects of the formation of the State Emergency Committee. Anatoli Lukyanov was unable to explain what duties were assigned to the commander-in-chief of the Baltic Military District Fyodor Kuzmin and recommended that this question be addressed to Vice-President of the USSR Gennadi Yanayev. Gorbunovs has not yet been able to contact the vice-president.

STATEMENT BY THE MEMORIAL SOCIETY
"This morning a coup d'etat has been carried out in the Soviet Union. Hiding behind slogans of consolidation, the conspirators are trying to erase the people's hope for the country's peaceful democratic development, to return it under the yoke of a totalitarian regime. The future of Russia and other republics is under a fatal threat. In this critical situation we call upon all fellow countrymen to rally around the legally elected democratic government, to support it in every way in its effort to restore law and order. The defence of the democratic choice of our people is the business of every citizen."

15.28. MIKHAIL GORBACHEV IS UNDER HOUSE ARREST
MOSCOW (RIA). According to reliable sources, President of the USSR Mikhail Gorbachev, removed from power on Aug. 19 by the State Emergency Committee "in connection with his inability to rule the country because of health problems", is now under house arrest at his dacha in the Crimea. The rumours that have been circulating since the morning of Aug. 19 about his death are apparently not true.

ALL! ALL! ALL!
The Coordinating Council of the Democratic Russia movement reports that a group of high-ranking plotters, having removed from power Gorbachev, Yeltsin and the legal government throughout the country, has carried out an attempted military coup which they are calling a "temporary state of emergency". We urge all industrial enterprises (with the exception of essential services) to stop working. The strike is to be unlimited, until the restoration of constitutional order. We urge to refrain from actions that would give the dictatorship a pretext for using force. We appeal to officers and soldiers of all branches of the military to replace commanders who obey the illegal orders of the rebels. Generals and officers who are loyal to your oath, take the initiative in your hands. Democrats, create civil disobedience committees everywhere. Party bureaucrats and generals who support the appalling adventurism are hoping to preserve their slipping powers and privileges. The people of Russia and other republics will wreck their plans! Coordinating Council of Democratic Russia.

15.41. STATE OF EMERGENCY, MOSCOW: ZIL AND KALIBR CONTINUE TO OPERATE

MOSCOW (RIA). "Reports that the ZIL works has gone on strike to protest the introduction of a state of emergency are untrue," Nikolai Misyutin, the duty person at ZIL told RIA by telephone. He added, "According to my information, the factory is working with great enthusiasm."

"All the shops of the Kalibr factory are working as usual, there is no talk of strike," Svetlana Chirkova, personal secretary of the factory's director told RIA by telephone.

OMSK (PF). 15.50 Moscow time. The streets are calm. There are no military patrols. At the daily Vecherny Omsk two KGB employees have been posted who are carrying out "strict control over the press". The publication in Omsk of the "Appeal to Citizens of Russia" is practically impossible. Local radio and television programmes have been cancelled. At 15.30 Moscow time a meeting of local and regional Democratic Russia activists was convened in the city Soviet building to discuss the creation of a committee to defend constitutional bodies. The chief of the local KGB Alexander Bannikov continues to assert that he knew nothing about the preparations for the change in leadership.

TYUMEN (PF). In the afternoon representatives of the regional Soviet conveyed to the regional committee the Appeal to Citizens of Russia by Yeltsin, Silayev and Khasbulatov. The appeal was read over local radio at 15.55 local time. The appeal is to be published in the Aug. 20 issue of Tyumenskiye izvestiya alongside with statements by the Union leaders.

15.51. STATE OF EMERGENCY, LENINGRAD: CHRONICLE OF AUGUST 19

LENINGRAD (RIA). RIA has learned that at Lenizdat publishers, where all city newspapers are being printed, no orders have been received to cancel any issue or ban any publication. Aug. 19 copies of the appeal of Russian President Boris Yeltsin to the people was printed.

Leningrad television told RIA that the only reports being received by the Fact TV station are from the RIA news agency. All television equipment in the TV centre were seized at 4.00 a.m. on Aug. 19 by persons in military uniform.

According to the Leningrad City Soviet press centre, the Leningrad Television Centre was being guarded by police units deployed on orders from Leningrad City Soviet Chairman Alexander Belyayev. A televised address by the chairman of the Leningrad City Soviet planned for 14.00 did not take place for unknown reasons.

The Leningrad police received word from Moscow that the Leningrad police is supposed to obey the Russian Ministry of the Interior. But high-ranking Leningrad police officials have refused to comment on this report.

15.56. KHABAROVSK TERRITORY AUTHORITIES POSSESS
SPARSE INFORMATION ON EVENTS IN MOSCOW

KHABAROVSK (RIA). The chief of the Khabarovsk KGB Vitali
Pirozhnyak told RIA that he has no information about what has happened
in Moscow other than what was reported on the radio. According to
Pirozhnyak, he has received no orders that his employees have been put on
combat alert. The same was said by the first deputy chief of the Political
Administration of the Far Eastern Military District Nikolai Maryanin. He
said that martial law would not be imposed without the knowledge of local
authorities.

Speaking on Khabarovsk television, Litvinov, chairman of the territorial executive committee and a member of the USSR parliament, urged the
population of the region to remain calm. He said that he possessed no
additional information on developments in Moscow. He also said that he
had ordered a round-the-clock watch to be organized at factories and
executive committees in order to ensure supplies of foodstuff to the
population and the operation of the municipal services.

IRKUTSK (PF). A meeting was held in the Irkutsk Regional Executive Committee at 16.00 at which the following resolution was adopted: 1.
To recognize the removal of the USSR President as illegal; to immediately
convene congresses of People's Deputies of the USSR and Russia; 2. To
obey the legally elected government of Russia and not obey the State
Emergency Committee.

Chairman of the Irkutsk Regional Executive Committee, Yuri
Nozhikov, speaking on regional television, read out the decrees of the
Russian President and the Regional Executive Committee's resolution and
urged residents of the region to obey the legal government of Russia and to
remain calm and show restraint. Yuri Nozhikov invited residents of the city
to take part in a rally in support of Boris Yeltsin scheduled for 18.00 on Aug.
20. According to Alexander Koshelyov, an aide to Russian Deputy Gennadi
Alekseyev, a committee for the defence of the legally elected government
was formed in Irkutsk.

19.07. EMERGENCY SITUATION, MOSCOW: ARMOURED VE-
HICLES OCCUPY APPROACHES TO MANEGE SQUARE

MOSCOW (RIA). By 17.00, APCs cleared the approaches to Manege
Square. Trolleybuses used by the demonstrators to stop movement along
Tverskaya Street have been cleared away, and armoured vehicles occupy all
the streets flowing into Manege Square. Movement of transport is impossible, but pedestrians wishing to get into the square are not stopped.

A general who did not give his name spoke from an APC asking the
crowd to disperse. But the crowd, which had thinned out after the departure
of some people for the Russian parliament building, began to grow again.

Xerox copies of Russian President Yeltsin's Appeal and Decree were dropped from the windows of the Moscow Soviet building in Tverskaya Street into the crowd below.

UFA (PF). Since the announcement of the beginning of the Emergency Committee's activities, everything has been relatively quiet in Bashkiria. There is no information about any strikes or rallies on the Bashkir territory. Returning from Moscow to Ufa in the evening of Aug. 19, Murtaz Rakhimov, Chairman of the Supreme Soviet of the Bashkir SSR, reported that a group of representatives of Russia's 15 former autonomous republics had been to see Gennadi Yanayev. Questioned by the leaders of the former autonomies, Yanayev said that a group of the country's leaders had approached Gorbachev at his Crimean retreat insisting that order be immediately restored in the country. To this, Gorbachev allegedly said: "I have a deputy, Yanayev, let him restore order." Representatives of the former autonomies told Yanayev that they would support the Emergency Committee provided the reforms followed the democratic course as before; they would categorically deny it any support if there was a danger of military dictatorship.

In Ufa, Deputy Chairman of the Bashkirian Council of Ministers Mansur Ayupov arrested the current issue of the republican youth paper *Leninets,* which has a circulation of 80,000 copies in the republic.

19.15. GENERAL STRIKE ANNOUNCED BY MINERS

MOSCOW (RIA). "The executive bureau of the Interrepublican Independent Trade Union of Miners had decided to go on an general indefinite strike in the Kuznetsk, Donetsk and Pechora coal-fields as of midnight Aug. 20," said Boris Utkin, chairman of the miners trade union executive council, people's deputy of the Russian Federation, and economic adviser to the Russian President. "This is a declaration of civil disobedience to the Emergency Committee. At the present moment, the question is being discussed of the miners of Sakhalin joining the strike."

A joint session of the Vorkuta workers' strike committee and the Vorkuta miners' independent trade unions carried an appeal to the miners and other workers of the Russian Federation and of Vorkuta to support the Russian President's decree of Aug. 19, and to begin, as of midnight Aug. 20, a strike in support of the legally elected authorities of the Russian Federation, and of the President of the Russian Federation.

19.18 IVAN SILAYEV'S INTERVIEW TO RIA CORRESPONDENT

MOSCOW (RIA). "Today, the fate of the Russian leadership in the coming days can be said to be completely uncertain," said Ivan Silayev, Chairman of the Council of Ministers of the Russian Federation. "We assume that any sort of situation is possible," he added in his interview to an RIA parliamentary correspondent. "We have neither tanks nor any other kind of weapons. But we have the Russian people's confidence, and I have no doubt that it will be precisely the Russian people who will speak out in defence of the human rights, of constitutional norms concerning both the USSR President and the President of Russia, as well as all the legally elected bodies."

"We are ready for anything," the Russian Prime Minister remarked. "Even if the worst happens--which is also a possibility--the citizens of Russia will have a kind word to say about us."

"In any case, the outcome of this adventuriest move is clear even today," Ivan Silayev stressed. "It can only be a complete failure for those who started it all."

CHELYABINSK (PF). On Aug. 19, deputies of the Chelyabinsk City Soviet representing the Democratic Russia movement held a rally in the city's main square. Vadim Solovyov, chairman of the city Soviet, told the rally that an extraordinary session of the presidium of the regional Soviet had confirmed that the city and the region upheld the Constitution and the laws of the Russian Federation.

KHABAROVSK (PF). All official Japanese delegations postponed their visits to the USSR citing the "situation in the country" as the reason. The police patrol the streets. A Khabarovsk TV announcer ended the broadeasts with this sentence: "No one knows what will happen tomorrow."

VLADIVOSTOK (PF). The Pacific Fleet is in a state of heightened alert. The city itself is quiet. No police are visible in public places. The leaders of the Primorye Territory have made no official statements.

MAGADAN (PF). Commercial TV has been closed down. State-run radio is broadcasting. The city is quiet. No patrols in the street. All the topmost leaders of the region are on leave. Military and police officials as well as KGB representatives refuse to comment on the situation.

BARNAUL (PF). Alexei Kuleshov, chairman of the Altai Territory Soviet, held a conference at which he instructed heads of departments and committees of the Territor Executive Committee to comply with the requirements of the state of emergency.

KEMEROVO (PF). An appeal from Yeltsin, Silayev, and Khasbulatov to the citizens of Russia was telephoned from Moscow to the council of workers' committees of Kuzbas. Tomorrow, it will be published in the local press. At 19.00 local time, an extraordinary session of the council of workers' committees of Kuzbas was held in Prokopievsk.

KAZAN (PF). The situation in the city's streets is normal. All enterprises as well as public transport and shops are working. No extra police patrols or military patrols are in evidence. A conference of the city's local administration departments, including the Interior Ministry department, was held at the city executive committee. A representative of the Kazan city committee of the CPSU was present at the conference, for the first time in recent months.

Some members of the Presidium of the Supreme Soviet of Tatarstan expressed concern about cancellation of presidential rule in the republic and a "return to the autonomous state". Some voiced the view that no changes would be implemented in Tatarstan because "Union rather than Russian laws were in effect here." Another view was also expressed: the Constitutions of the USSR and the Russian Federation still being unchanged, Tatarstan would now unquestionably remain within Russia. The arrival of Mintimer Shaimiyev, President of Tatarstan, was expected from Moscow. A session of the Presidential Council of the Tatar SSR was appointed for Aug. 20.

NABEREZHNYE CHELNY (PF). According to various sources, the situation in the city is quiet. The presidium of the city Soviet conducted a conference of the city departments including the KGB, the Interior, and the public procurator's office. The city authorities had no information except that officially broadcast on the radio.

YELABUGA (PF). The city is quiet; no sign of heightened activity. Trade union and Party committees of major plants express the hope that the Emergency Committee's measures will be received with understanding and even, probably, with approval.

19.23. THE POSITION OF DEMOCRATIC PRESS CRITICAL

MOSCOW (RIA). As reported to RIA by a *Moscow News* worker, the printers, refused today to print the papers *Moscow News, Moskovsky Komsomolets, Rossiyskaya gazeta, Nezavisimaya gazeta, Kuranty,* and perhaps some others. He said that the printers had offered no explanation on whose orders they refused to print *Moscow News.*

"The editorial board of the paper *Grazhdanskoye dostoinstvo,* the organ of the Constitutional Democrats' Party, has been evacuated and has gone underground," Victor Zolotaryov, chairman of the CDP, told RIA.

19.28. ANATOLI SOBCHAK: SPEECH AT SESSION OF LENINGRAD CITY SOVIET

LENINGRAD (RIA). On his return from Moscow, Anatoli Sobchak spoke at an extraordinary session of the Leningrad Soviet of People's Deputies. He said that he had met members of the Emergency Committee and regarded them as "criminals who would have to be punished". Anatoli Sobchak also stated that, according to information available to him USSR President Mikhail Gorbachev had been told to resign, which he had refused to do, demanding that he be allowed to speak on TV.

MOSCOW (PF). The Supreme Council of the Liberal Democratic Party of the Soviet Union declared its "complete support for the transition of the entire authority throughout the territory of the USSR to the State Committee for the State of Emergency, and for the restoration of the authority of the Constitution throughout the country" (TASS, Aug. 19).

19.32. LIVE BROADCASTING BLOCKED ON LENINGRAD TV
LENINGRAD (RIA). Live broadcasting from the Leningrad TV centre is being blocked on orders from Moscow. This was stated by Yuri Vdovin, chairman of the Leningrad Soviet's commission on glasnost, who tried without success to speak on Leningrad TV on Aug. 19.

Nevertheless, as an RIA correspondent was told at the Leningrad Soviet press centre, Boris Petrov, chairman of the Leningrad committee for television and radio, promised to make it technically possible for deputies of the Leningrad Soviet's extraordinary session to appear in a live programme.

SEOUL (PF). Immediately on hearing reports of the changes in the USSR, an urgent conference was called of the Ministry for Commerce and Industry and of the Council for Economic Planning of the Republic of Korea. They considered the possible effect of the events in Moscow on the future of the $ 3,000 million credit which the South Korean government promised the USSR. (TASS, Aug. 19).

TOKYO (PF). The Tokyo Exchange reacted to the events in the USSR with a drastic fall in share prices. At closing time, the Nikkei Index-- the average index of the price of the shares of 225 leading companies--fell by 1.357.67 points.

The price of the yen sharply fell, too, at the Tokyo Currency Exchange. Today, trading at the Exchange ended at $ 1 = 138.4 yen (TASS, Aug. 19).

PARIS (PF). The Foreign Ministry of France has issued the following statement: "Mikhail Gorbachev's deposition, if it is finally confirmed, is an important event, the more so that it is followed by the introduction of the state of emergency. To assess the significance of this event both for the USSR and for international relations, further information is needed on the circumstances in which this deposition took place, and, most importantly, on the measures which those who effected the deposition will take" (TASS, Aug. 19).

19.43. KEMEROVO REGIONAL SOVIET DOES NOT RECOGNIZE STATE EMERGENCY COMMITTEE
KEMEROVO (RIA). The Kemerovo Regional Soviet does not recognize the Emergency Committee. Head of the Kemerovo department of the Interior Gen. Nikolai Shkurat announced that he had given orders to the Kemerovo police not to interfere with the holding of rallies.

*On August 19th, Boris Nikolajevitch Yeltsin climbed on top of tank number 110 of the Taman division and told the citizens of Russia that they were dealing with a right-wing, reactionary, unconstitutional Putsch!*

*Because of his courageous and drastic (energetic, vigorous) actions during the Putsch, Boris Yeltsin, president of the CIS, gained immense popularity.*

*Moscow, August 19th, 5:10 pm.*
*Tanks and armoured vehicles tried to cross the Borodinski bridge direction city centre. They were stopped by demonstrators, resulting in this fraternization.*

*Russian Vice-President Alexander Rutzkoj speaks from the balcony of the "White House". He participated in the war in Afghanistan.*

*Leningrad. Leaders and members of the labour union of the production department o fthe Kirov factories are sending a telegram and writing support for Russian President Boris Yeltsin, the mayor of Leningrad Anatoli Sobchak and the chairman of Leningrad city council Alexander Beljajev.*

A spontaneous rally was held in Kemerovo at which Yeltsin's Appeal and Decree were read out. The rally was held under police protection. A similar rally was called in Prokopievsk. In all likelihood, Kemerovo miners will go on strike as of Aug. 20. Unconfirmed reports say that the troops of the Siberian military district are confined to barracks, and all leaves have been cancelled.

**19.46. GAMSAKHURDIA CALLS FOR CALM**
TBILISI (RIA). President of Georgia Zviad Gamsakhurdia has called on the citizens of the republic to stay calm and not to leave their workplaces. Hundreds of people awaiting news from Moscow have gathered in front of Georgia's Government House. There are no reports of any movement of fresh troops into Georgia.

**20.06. STATE OF EMERGENCY, NIZHNY NOVGOROD: ATTEMPT TO SET UP AN EMERGENCY COMMISSION FALLS**
NIZHNY NOVGOROD (RIA). Alexander Sokolov, Chairman of the Nizhny Novgorod Regional Soviet, made an attempt on Aug. 19 to set up a regional emergency commission including officials from the KGB, the Interior Ministry and the Army. His efforts were blocked by radically minded deputies of the regional and city Soviets.

On Aug. 19, a rally was held in Minin and Pozharsky Square in Nizhny Novgorod at which the latest decrees of Boris Yeltsin, President of the Russian Federation, and his appeal ''To the Citizens of Russia'' were read out. An extraordinary session of the Nizhny Novgorod city Soviet is planned for the morning of Aug. 21.

**20.08. STATE OF EMERGENCY, LENINGRAD: RALLY IN ST. ISAAC'S SQUARE**
LENINGRAD (RIA). A protest rally under the slogan ''No the Fascism!'' was held in St. Isaac's Square in Leningrad. Mayor Anatoly Sobchak's speech at an extraordinary session of the Leningrad Soviet was broadcast on the radio. Barricades are being built out of construction flat vans, trolleybuses and park benches. An RIA report was read out at the rally to say that no state of emergency would be introduced in Kazakhstan, which was greeted with stormy applause.

According to a report from the press centre of the Leningrad department of the KGB, the introduction of the state of emergency was a surprise to many KGB officers. The press centre withheld from any official comment but, according to some reports, the personal attitude of many security officers to the Emergency Committee is negative.

20.15. FEDERATION OF INDEPENDENT TRADE UNIONS CALLS EMERGENCY SESSION OF ITS COUNCIL

MOSCOW (RIA). The leaders of the Russian trade unions from various industries gathering today in Moscow called for an emergency session of the council of the Federation of Independent Trade Unions of the RSFSR on Aug. 21-22, to define the position of the trade union centre on the situation in the country.

TOMSK (PF). The presidiums of the Tomsk regional and city Soviets declared the Emergency Committee to be illegal. It has been decided to publish the Appeal of the leadership of Russia and the Decree of the Russian President.

IZHEVSK (PF). On Aug. 19, the Presidium of the Supreme Soviet of Udmurtia held several sessions. A resolution was passed placing the responsibility for the situation in the republic on the Supreme Soviet and the Soviet government bodies in the republic's cities and districts. No setting up of any emergency commissions is to be permitted on the territory of Udmurtia.

ROSTOV-ON-DON (PF). A speaker for the public relations section of the Rostov regional KGB department told PF that officers of the Rostov KGB had learned of the introduction of the state of emergency in the country from a radio broadcast. ''We don't know what we are to do,'' he said. ''The teletypes are silent. We are awaiting orders from Moscow.''

20.13. STATE OF EMERGENCY, MOSCOW: RUSSIAN DEPUTIES INTEND TO SPEAK TO THE MILITARY

MOSCOW (RIA). The Russian Deputies representing Moscow and the Moscow Region intend to go to the military units stationed in Moscow to inform the soldiers and officers of the Appeal ''To the Citizens of Russia'' and the latest decrees of Boris Yeltsin, President of the Russian Federation. The decision of Russia's President and government will be broadcast to the citizenry through leaflets at Moscow's railways and airports. The capital's four airports have been divided between parliamentary committees.

The leaders of the republic will appear every hour before the Muscovites who have gathered round the Russian parliament building. A speech by Boris Yeltsin is expected at 20.00.

Gennadi Burbulis, State Secretary of the Russian Federation, said that many enterprises in Moscow, Sverdlovsk and Leningrad have already gone on strike. In the morning, groups of Russian Deputies will go to Moscow's major plants and factories. In Burbulis's words, the ''senselessness of the coup'' must be proved during 24 hours.

20.39. STATE OF EMERGENCY, LENINGRAD: POLITICAL STRIKE
PLANNED FOR AUGUST 20

LENINGRAD (RIA). Anatoli Sobchak, Mayor of Leningrad, said
that a political strike and an act of civil disobedience will be held on Aug.
20 in Leningrad. Only the services ensuring the city's life support system
will not go on strike. Anatoli Sobchak also called on Leningraders to come
on Aug. 20 to Palace Square, and to defend freedom in orderly fashion.

20.41. TWO MEMBERS OF PRESIDIUM OF SUPREME SOVIET OF
RUSSIA VOTE AGAINST CALLING OF EMERGENCY SESSION OF
PARLIAMENT

MOSCOW (RIA). At a session of the presidium of the Supreme
Soviet of Russia held on Aug. 19, Boris Isayev, deputy chairman of the
Supreme Soviet of the Russian Federation, and Vladimir Isakov, head of the
Russian parliament's Soviet of the Republic, voted against the resolution of
call an emergency session of the Supreme Soviet of the Russian Federation.
Another member of the Presidium, Yuri Voronin, chairman of the parliamentary commission on budget, plans, taxes and prices, abstained. An RIA
correspondent heard this today from Boris Isayev. He explained his action
by arguing that a position on such an important issue as the present situation
in the country could only be defined after a careful study of all the facts.

20.44. LEADER OF THE POPULAR FRONT OF LATVIA ON COUP IN
THE USSR

RIGA (RIA). Despite a military threat, Latvia's Supreme Soviet, the
republic's government and the local government bodies must continue to
work in accordance with the laws of the Latvian Republic, said Romualdas
Rajukas, chairman of the Popular Front of Latvia. In his speech on the radio,
he informed the population of the results of the emergency session of the
PFL's board.

''If the work of the Supreme Soviet or the republic's government is
interfered with,'' he remarked, ''a campaign of civil disobedience must be
started. Local power must be in the hands of the local government bodies.
Simultaneously, all the sections of the Popular Front of Latvia must
envigorate their activity. Coordinative and reserve centres of administration
must be set up. The campaign of civil disobedience will begin the moment
the broadcasts of the Latvian radio or TV are interrupted, or they begin
broadcasting in accordance with the interests of the opposition,'' Romualdas
Rajukas said.

Quoting the information service of the government of Latvia, Lieta
agency reported that at 19.00 an OMON unit occupied the Latvian TV
centre. According to unconfirmed reports, there were no casualties.

20.47. PRESIDIUM OF ALL-UNION COUNCIL OF SERVICEMEN'S PARENTS SUPPORTS APPEAL OF RUSSIAN GOVERNMENT

MOSCOW (RIA). Presidium of the All-Union Council of Servicemen's Parents has called on the country's citizens and the world community to speak out in support of the Russian government's Appeal.

"We, soldiers' mothers, members of the All-Union Council of Servicemen's Parents, call on you, officers, soldiers, seamen, ensigns, on all servicemen of the USSR Armed Forces, to show great civic spirit and restraint in this difficult situation. Do not take part in the coup," said the appeal.

20.49. IVAN SILAYEV'S INTERVIEW TO *ROSSIYA*

MOSCOW (RIA). "We could not expect this sort of development," said Ivan Silayev, Chairman of the Council of Ministers of the Russian Federation, in an interview granted to the *Rossiya newspaper.* "It was all the more unexpected since it occurred on the eve of an event of major significance for Russia and for all the sovereign republics--the signing of the Union Treaty."

"In the morning I conducted a session of the Council of Ministers of the Russian Federation," the Prime Minister Continued. "I told the ministers at the very beginning: each of you must define your position; you must make your choice. There was unanimous support for the acts of the Russian government and a readiness to act in accordance with the laws and the Constitution."

"We shall not budge, we shall do everything we can to defend our freedom, we shall not betray our people, whatever it may cost us. We have no weapons, no tanks, guns or canon. But we count on the support of Russians, and we belive that reaction will fail!" concluded Ivan Silayev.

DONETSK (PF). According to Victor Bychkov, first Deputy Chairman of the City Soviet, the Donetsk Interior department are placed on high alert, although there were no orders for this from their chiefs in the Interior Ministry. Soviet Army units on the city territory received no instructions, directives, orders or resolutions from the headquarters of the military district. The city Soviet received no information from the KGB.

20.52. STATE OF EMERGENCY, MOSCOW: RALLY AT RUSSIA'S PARLIAMENT BUILDING

MOSCOW (RIA). In the evening of Aug. 19 Boris Yeltsin spoke to a rally of many thousands at the Russian Federation's parliament building. The Russian President told the gathering about the latest decisions of the Russian leadership. He also announced that Russia's leaders would stay permanently in the parliament building.

21.05. MOSCOW (RIA). Dear Colleagues!

Record, document and remember everything that happens to you and around you in these tragic hours. Otherwise our readers, radio listeners and televiewers will be told tomorrow that the coup was no coup at all but an action for stabilizing the situation in the country misinterpreted by journalists; that the commodities and the foodstuffs promised by the armed rescuers of the communist dream are not the result of the sabotage that has undermined the situation in the last few months but a great boon that has descended on us due to the wisdom of the Party and military leadership.

If we do not show ourselves to be professionals in the true meaning of this word, we shall never become ones--despite the fact that the present coup is doomed.

Andrei Vinogradov,
*President of the Russian Information Agency*

21.35. MOLDOVA'S POPULAR FRONT PROTESTS AGAINST COUP IN MOSCOW

KISHINEV (RIA). At an emergency session, the Popular Front of Moldova passed two appeals today: "To the Romanians of the World" and "To the Population of the Republic". The appeals state that a coup has been carried out in Moscow and that power has been seized by reactionary forces planning to put an end to democratic reforms.

The appeal to the republic's population calls on the citizens to occupy Kishinev's central square and to protect government buildings and the radio and TV centre. According to Mikhaj Taske, secretary of the People's Front of Moldova, more than a hundred people responded to the appeal and went patrolling the streets together with the republic's OMON. According to other leaders of this social and political movement, directives to control military units have been sent to all the regional departments of the Popular Front. It is suggested that they report all movements of army units to the Popular Front headquarters.

At 21.00, a rally was called on Great National Assembly Square in Kishinev by the People's Front of Moldova. According to Mikhaj Taske, dozens of thousands of people gathered in the square. A session was also held in Kishinyov of the Alliance for the Republic's National Independence uniting 14 democratic parties and movements, which also expressed a negative attitude to the latest events.

21.40. EXECUTIVE COMMITTEES IN MOSCOW REFUSE TO CARRY OUT ORDERS FROM THE EMERGENCY COMMITTEE

MOSCOW (RIA). Anatoli Manokhin and Altai Picheol, people's deputies of the Russian Federation, told RIA that the executive committees of some of the local Soviets in the capital have refused to carry out the orders of the Emergency Committee.

21.59. TV APPEARANCE OF LENINGRAD'S LEADERS
	LENINGRAD (RIA). In the evening of Aug. 19, Leningrad's Mayor Anatoly Sobchak appeared on Leningrad TV to read he latest decrees of the President of Russia. Vice-Mayor Vyacheslav Shcherbakov and Chairman of the Leningrad Regional Soviet Yuri Yarov, speaking after him, stated that they had been included in the regional emergency committee without their knowledge. Yuri Yarov called on the population of the province not to stop work in the fields, and asked Leningrad Regional Soviet deputies to ensure normal functioning of the regional legislative organs.
	SURGUT (PF). Victor Tsives, chairman of the exchange board of the Surgut commodity and raw materials exchange, called Gorbachev's removal an attempt at a military coup.
	VORKUTA (PF). The Vorkuta city workers' striking committee and the independent trade union of the miners of Vorkuta passed an appeal to the citizens of the Russian Federation and the workers of Vorkuta. the striking committee called on the miners and other workers of the city to "support the appeal of Boris Yeltsin, President of the Russian Federation, and to go on a strike of protest as of midnight Aug. 20 in support of the legally elected organs of power of the Russian Federation and of the President of the USSR."
	PERF (PF). At 22.00, 96 deputies of the Perm City Soviet gathered at the state executive committee conference hall to declare unanimously their decision to call an emergency session of the city Soviet at 18.00 on Aug. 20. Perm City Soviet deputies fully supported the Russian government but put off their decision until Aug. 20, having failed to secure a quorum on Aug. 19; besides, the session was held in the absence of the chairmen of the city Soviet and the city executive committee.

22.01. KIROV PLANT SUPPORTS YELTSIN'S DECREES, IS READY FOR ACTS OF CIVIL DISOBEDIENCE
	LENINGRAD (RIA). The meeting of trade union activists and workers' committee of the Kirov Plant production combine sent a telegram of support to Russian President Boris Yeltsin, Mayor of Leningrad Anatoli Sobchak, and Chairman of the Leningrad Soviet Alexander Belyaev.
	Simultaneously a telegram was sent to USSR Vice-President Gennady Yanayev demanded that a chance be given "for the legally elected USSR President Gorbachev and Russian Federation Yeltsin" to speak on TV and radio until noon, Aug. 20. If this was not done, said the telegram, the workers of the Kirov Plant reserved the right to "call on labour collectives to begin a campaign of civil disobedience to the illegally created committees."

22.03. LATVIAN REPUBLIC'S INTERIOR MINISTRY BUILDING SEIZED IN RIGA

RIGA (RIA). According to information received by a RIA reporter from the Latvian government's press service, at about 21.00, Aug. 20, a unit of the Riga OMON seized the building of the Latvian republic's Interior Ministry.

22.06. UNIT OF TAMAN DIVISION TO GUARD SUPREME SOVIET OF Russian FEDERATION

MOSCOW (RIA). The radio station of the Supreme Soviet of the Russian Federation, set up in the evening of Aug. 19, broadcast about 22.00 Moscow time an announcement read by People's Deputy Victor Mironov. He asked the Muscovites who had gathered to guard the Russian parliament building to dismantle the barricades to make a passage for one of the units of the Taman division, commanded by Major Sergei Yevdokimov. According to Mironov, this unit, true to its oath of allegiance and the Russian people, will place its ten tanks to cover the approaches to the "White House" to stop the storming of the seat of the republican organs of authority expected during the night of the 19/20 of August.

22.20. YELENA BONNER CALLS ON MUSCOVITES TO "DEFEND FREEDOM"

MOSCOW (RIA). Yelena Bonner, Academician Sakharov's widow and well-known civil rights fighter, has called on Muscovites to "defend the Russian government and the Russian President," and also the President of the USSR. "Today we must prove," Yelena Bonner said, "that we deserve our name of the people of the capital, that we are more than just a mob concerned with buying sausage."

22.26. STATE OF EMERGENCY, MOSCOW: TANKS AT RUSSIA'S PARLIAMENT BUILDING

MOSCOW (RIA). An armoured company of the Taman Guards Division has just arrived at the White House. The arrival of ten tanks led by Maj. Sergei Yevdokimov was greeted with triumphal applause from many thousands of Muscovites who had gathered at the seat of the Russian leadership to protect it against a possible attack.

23.04. TYUMEN REGIONAL SOVIET: SETTING UP OF THE EMERGENCY COMMITTEE UNCONSTITUTIONAL

TYUMEN (RIA--RADIO RUSSIA). An emergency session of the presidium of the Regional Soviet of People's Deputies has passed a resolution declaring the setting up of the Emergency Committee to be unconstitutional. The Soviet has called on institutions of state power on the territory of Tyumen province, supervisory and law and order bodies and heads of plants and factories to ensure compliance with the decrees of the President of the Russian Federation. In an interview granted to the local radio station, the chairman of the Tyumen Regional Soviet demanded the dissolution of the Emergency Committee.

**23.06. AFGHAN WAR VETERANS OF TOMSK TO WORK OUT THEIR POSITION ON AUGUST 20**

TOMSK (RIA--RADIO RUSSIA). Chairman of the Tomsk Regional Soviet of People's Deputies has declared that the legally elected bodies, the regional Soviet and its structures, are in authority in the province. The introduction of the state of emergency is unconstitutional and unjustified by the existing situation. The Soviet is in control of the situation at present. A permanent watch has been set up at the Soviet. However, the first leader of the province has called on the population to refrain from strikes until the situation cleared. On Aug. 20, Afghan war veterans will gather at the city Soviet to define their position.

**23.08. YELTSIN'S DECREES WILL BE CARRIED OUT IN VORONEZH**

VORONEZH (RIA--RADIO RUSSIA). Victor Kalashnikov, chairman of the Voronezh Regional Soviet, has stated that he will unconditionally comply with Yeltsin's decrees. On Aug. 19, two rallies were held here. Law enforcement bodies take a neutral stance. The fax link between the regional executive committee and Russia's Supreme Soviet is disrupted. The leaders of the region cannot receive any directives from Moscow.

**23.16. TEREK COSSACKS SUPPORT CENTRAL GOVERNMENT'S MEASURES**

MOSCOW (RIA). "The Terek Cossacks support the central government's measures to stabilize the socio-political situation in the country," said Vasily Konyakhin, ataman (chieftain) of the Terek Cossacks. A telegram to this effect, approved on Aug. 19 at a session of the board of Terek Cossacks, was sent to Gennady Yanayev, who has assumed the post of the country's acting President. "The campaign of the Emergency Committee is regarded as the first step towards the stabilization of the economic, social and political situation in the country," stated Vassili Konyakhin in a telephone interview to an RIA correspondent. Vassily Konyakhin is the ataman of the Grand Circle of the Terek Cossacks, which has three divisions in Northern Ossetia and one in Chechen-Ingushetia and Kabarda-Balkaria each--the Caucasian republics which form part of Russia.

23.18. APPEAL OF RSFSR VICE-PRESIDENT ALEXANDER RUT-
SKOI TO SERVICEMEN

MOSCOW (RIA). "Comrades! Friends! An attempt is made in this country to achieve a military coup to establish a military dictatorship of the Stalinist type. State leaders responsible for the preset situation in the country, aware of their impending defeat and inevitable calling to account by the people, have mounted an anti-Constitutional plot. The Emergency Committee that they have set up plunges the country into the horrors of internecine strife--using you as an instrument. Comrades! I, an officer of the Soviet Army, a colonel, a Hero of the Soviet Union, I who have travelled the flaming roads of Afghanistan, who have known the horrors of war, call on you, my comrades, officers, soldiers and seamen, not to fight against the people, against your fathers, mothers, brothers and sisters. I appeal to your honour, your reason, and your heart. Today, the fate of the country, the fate of her free and democratic development is in our hands.

"Do not permit bloodshed! No support to the plotters. Do everything you can to thwart their criminal plans. I call on you to take the side of the legally elected institutions of power, the President of the Russian Federation and the Council of Ministers of the Russian Federation.

Alexander Rutskoi,
Vice-President of the Russian Federation,
*Hero of the Soviet Union.*"

23.24. DECREE OF PRESIDENT OF RUSSIAN SOVIET FEDERATIVE SOCIALIST REPUBLIC, AUG. 19

MOSCOW (RIA). Considering the situation as it is now, I decree that O.I. Lobov, First Deputy of the Chairman of the Council of Ministers of the Russian Federation, A.V. Lobov, member of the State Council of the Russian Federation, S.N. Krasavchenko, member of the Presidium of the Supreme Soviet of the Russian Federation, should organize operative management of the republic's economy and, in case of need, ensure effective functioning of the basic state structures.

To carry out these tasks, I authorize them to enlist the cooperation of the necessary officials in the name of the President of the RSFSR.

All organizations on the territory of the Russian Federation shall cooperate with the aforementioned officials.

Boris Yeltsin
President of RSFSR
Moscow, Kremlin
*August 19, 1991, 17.30*

23.26. RYAZAN WILL NOT OBEY THE EMERGENCY COMMITTEE

RYAZAN (RIA). Information on the introduction of the state of emergency in Ryazan reached RIA in the morning of Aug. 19. On the same day, an RIA correspondent phoned Valeri Ryumin, Mayor of the city, who reported that members of an emergency commission had visited him in the morning. Ryazan leader had called them criminals and kicked them our of his office. He also said that Sergei Ponomaryov, head of the Ryazan School of the Interior, had also declared his loyalty to the Russian authorities, as had the head of the regional KGB department Yuri Chichelov who said that he would act in accordance with the laws of the Russian Federation and the republic's constitution. According to Ryumin, head of the local department of the Interior avoided meeting him under various pretexts.

Ryazan's Mayor also reported that the decrees of Russian President Boris Yeltsin were read out on the PA system from the Mayor's House. It was also from here that they were passed on by telephone to 30 regional centres of Russia. 20,000 copies of the Russian President's Decree and various leaflets have been printed and distributed at the city's plants and factories.

23.30. STATE OF EMERGENCY, MOLDOVA: GOVERNMENT'S DECLARATION ADOPTED

KISHINEV (RIA). The removal from power of the legally elected USSR President is an unconstitutional coup d'etat organized by reactionary forces, states a declaration of the government of Moldova approved at a joint session of the republic's government and the presidium of parliament on Aug. 19. This was reported by the Moldova-Press agency. All decisions of the so-called State Committee for the State of Emergency are illegal and invalid on the republic's territory, the Declaration says. Only legally elected bodies--parliament, the president and the government of the republic as well as the local government bodies--function in the Republic of Moldova.

**AUGUST 20TH, 1991**

00.00. ALL QUIET IN KUZBAS: PREPARATIONS FOR STRIKE

KUZBAS (RIA--RADIO RUSSIA). Everything is quiet in the Kuzbas cities of the coal-field region. An appeal from the presidium of the regional al Soviet of people's deputies to the people of Kuzbas states that the presidium viewed the events as an attempt at a coup d'etat, and called on the population of the region not to comply with the orders and directives of the Emergency Committee.

In response to the Russian leadership's appeal, the workers' committees of Kuzbas decided to go on an indefinite strike. The Raspadskaya mine, the largest in the area, has already declared its readiness; it will be joined by others. An appeal from workers' committees stated they did not recognize the self-proclaimed Emergency Committee. In the evening, a numerous rally was held in Kemerovo.

VORKUTA (PF). Five out of the thirteen mines of the Vorkutaugol Combine went on a protest strike as of midnight Aug. 20. The Vorkuta city workers' strike committee announced that three more mines stopped work before noon, Aug. 20 (in all, eight mines were on strike). According to the city strike committee, the remaining five mines of the Vorkutaugol would join the strikers before the end of the day.

00.04. STATE OF EMERGENCY, NOVOSIBIRSK: REGIONAL SO-VIET RECOGNIZES GOVERNMENT OF RUSSIA ONLY

NOVOSIBIRSK (RIA). A session of the presidium of the City Soviet passed a decision not to recognize the Emergency Committee, and to obey the decrees of the President of Russia. The Deputies instructed the mass media to report the decision to the citizens, but Communist Party publishing houses refused Sibirskaya gazeta and Molodost Sibiri a chance to publish a joint special issue. But the papers will be printed by an underground plant. There are no troops in the city.

00.08. KRASNOYARSK WAITS FOR CONFIRMATION OF YELTSIN'S DECREES THROUGH OFFICIAL CHANNELS

KRASNOYARSK (RIA). A session of the presidium of the territorial Soviet decided not to publish in the papers or broadcast on the radio and TV decrees by Boris Yeltsin, President of the Russian Federation. The deputies gave as the reason for their decision the fact that the texts of the decrees had not come through official channels. No troops are observed in the city.

00.10. KRASNODAR AUTHORITIES REFUSE TO OBEY YELTSIN'S DECREES

KRASNODAR (RIA). In the evening of Aug. 19, the coordinative council of the Democratic Russia local organization held a meeting. An appeal was adopted to the population of the Kuban region to support the Decrees of the President of Russia, and to join in the All-Russia indefinite strike. A rally is planned for 9.00 a.m., Aug. 20, near the building of the territorial executive committee.

Today, several Russian Deputies and city and regional Soviets' Deputies of democratic orientation met Nikolai Kondratenko, chairman of the territorial Soviet. The latter refused to obey any decrees of the President of Russia shown to him by the Deputies. He said that until these documents reached him through official channels he would not be guided by them. If the decrees arrived in the prescribed order, the presidium of the territorial Soviet would consider them.

00.15. ARMY DID NOT UNCONDITIONALLY SUPPORT NEW LEADERSHIP OF USSR: DOES THIS MEAN A SPLIT?

MOSCOW (RIA). According to information described to RIA as having been received "from reliable sources", several motorized rifle divisions from the Moscow region had orders to enter Moscow during the day of Aug. 19, but their commanders refused to obey these orders from the new authority. They declared that they would not shot at the people. Only the Kantemir Division was brought into Moscow. According to the same sources, there was wavering now in the Emergency Committee. After President Boris Yeltsin's Decree declaring this regional organ to be unconstitutional, representatives of Gennadi Yanayev, Acting President of the USSR, arrived at the Russian leadership's residency for talks. Information about vacillation in the leadership of the Army, the Interior Ministry and the KGB is reaching RIA. According to Alexander Muzykantsky, deputy premier of the Moscow government, interviewed by our correspondent, he had conversations with a number of generals on Aug. 19. To many of them, the events of Aug. 19 were unexpected, and they did not want to confront the people.

## 00.24. PARATROOPERS FROM TULA ARRIVED IN MOSCOW TO DEFEND RUSSIAN PARLIAMENT

MOSCOW (RIA). A company of paratroopers from the Tula Airborne Division with ten armoured vehicles arrived at about 23.00, Aug. 19, at the building of the Supreme Soviet of the Russian Federation to take part in the defence of the residency of the Russian authorities. According to the soldiers of the unit interviewed by an RIA reporter, they took the people's side and intended to prevent the "Lithuanian variant" happening in Russia. RIA correspondent reports form the building of the Russian parliament that Maj. Gen. Lebed, deputy commander-in-chief of the USSR Airborne Troops for battle training, arrived with this unit. Fearing a provocation, the Russian authorities did not permit the unit to approach the parliament building, and started negotiations with the general. According to unconfirmed reports, Lt. Gen. Grachev, commander-in-chief of the USSR Airborne Forces, is under house arrest in his office at the headquarters. So far there is no information on who ordered the arrest.

## 00.33. MOSCOW'S HOSPITALS PREPARE TO RECEIVE WOUNDED

MOSCOW (RIA). The Russian parliament radio service has broadcast the news that the toxic cases and intensive care units of some hospitals, including the Sklifosovsky clinic, are now ready to receive possible casualties. The doctors have recommended the Muscovites surrounding the parliament building to have wet handkerchiefs ready, and to use them to protect mouth and nose in case chemical agents are used.

## 00.33. RUTSKOI CALLS ON COMMUNISTS TO DISTANCE THEMSELVES FROM PUTSCHISTS

MOSCOW (RIA). Alexander Rutskoi, chairman of the council of the Democratic Party of the Communists of Russia (DPCR), called on the country's communists "not to obey the orders of the usurpers". On behalf of the DPCR, he demanded, in a declaration just published, that the CPSU Central Committee "immediately distance itself from the putschists whose ringleaders are members of the Communist Party and of its leading organs". Rutskoi also proposed that all groups and trends in the CPSU "forget their differences and defend the legally elected institutions of power jointly with other democratic forces".

MOSCOW (PF). In a statement broadcast by the interior radio service of the Russian parliament, Victor Utkin, chairman of the Independent Miners Union, says that, according to information available at 1.00 a.m., miners are on strike in Mezhdurechensk (two mines), Severodvinsk (six mines and two mine-building combines), Prokopyevsk (six mines plus workers of the car depot servicing the opencast colliery), Belov (several mines have begun laying-up operations and will stop work in the morning of Aug. 20), Novokuznetsk (three mines and two mine-building combines), Kiselevsk (one mine; four mines have begun laying-up operations and are expected to finish them before morning; one car depot is also not working), and Vorkuta (five mines). On the whole, according to Utkin, 40 enterprises are on strike, with 1,500 workmen at each, on average. Utkin also said that the miners of Soligorsk in Belorussia had also decided to go on strike. At one o'clock in the morning, members of the Russian Balloon Group fixed a balloon at the height of about 150 metres above the building of the Russian parliament, with the Russia's tricolour suspended from it.

01.48. RUSSIA'S BUSINESS CIRCLES RECOGNIZE LEGALLY ELECTED AUTHORITY

MOSCOW (RIA). On Aug. 19, a meeting was held of representatives of the Moscow business circles. It discussed the situation created by the coming to power of the Emergency Committee , and passed a resolution condemning ''an attempt at a coup d'etat''.

''Recognizing legally constituted authority, the laws of the USSR and of the Union republics, the right of peoples to self-determination, and supporting the Appeal of the Russian Federation's leadership to the citizens of Russia, the congress of Russian business circles is calling on all who hold the fate of their Motherland dear to be guided in their activities by the laws adopted by the authority elected by the people,'' says the statement.

''We call on the soldiers and officers of the Army, the KGB and the Interior Ministry not to become mere instruments in the hands of ambitious politicians. Your hands hold terrible weapons, but they must not be turned against your own people. Much innocent blood has been shed in the history of this country. It is your task to prevent it being shed again.''

Representatives of Russian business circles demanded an ''immediate convening of an emergency Congress of the People's Deputies of the USSR''.

01.54. DECREE OF BORIS YELTSIN, PRESIDENT OF RUSSIA

MOSCOW (RIA). Having carried out a coup d'etat and forcibly removed from power the USSR President and Supreme Commander-in-Chief of the Armed Forces, USSR Vice-President Gennadi I. Yanayev, Prime Minister Valentin S. Pavlov, Chairman of the USSR KGB Vladimir A. Kryuchkov, USSR Interior Minister Boris K. Pugo, USSR Defence Minister Dmitri T. Yazov, Chairman of the Peasants Union Vassili L. Starodubtsev, Oleg D. Baklanov, first deputy chairman of the State Committee for Defence, Alexander I. Tizyakov, president of the Industry, Construction and Communications Association, and their accomplices have committed the gravest crimes against the state, violating Article 62 of the Constitution of the USSR, Articles 64, 69, 70, 70' and 72 of the Criminal

Code of the Russian Federation and the corresponding articles of the Fundamentals of Criminal Legislation of the USSR and of the Union republics.

Having betrayed the people, the Motherland and the Constitution, they placed themselves outside the law.

In view of the above I decree that workers of the public prosecutors' offices, of the Committees for State Security and the Interior Ministries of the USSR and Russia, and servicemen aware of their responsibility for the fate of the people and the state and rejecting dictatorship, civil war and bloodshed, have the right to act in accordance with the Constitution and Laws of the USSR and Russia. As President of Russia, I promise you, in the name of the people who elected me, legal protection and moral support. The fate of the Union and of Russia is in your hands.

*Boris Yeltsin, President of Russia,*
*Moscow, Kremlin*
*August 19, 1991*
*22.30*

02.30. UKRAINE: SESSION OF PRESIDIUM OF SUPREME SOVIET TO BE HELD ON AUGUST 20. COUP ATTEMPT EXPECTED TO BE CONDEMNED

KIEV (RIA). A session of the presidium of the Ukraine's Supreme Soviet, planned for late Aug. 19, was postponed because of failure to secure a quorum. It is now planned for 10.00 a.m., Aug. 20. According to sources in the Ukrainian capital, a resolution is expected condemning the attempted coup. A meeting of the opposition's People's Rada, appointed for 11.00, is also expected to pass a resolution condemning the setting up of the State Emergency Committee. According to sources in Kiev, the army shows no activity at all here, although the commander of the Kiev Military District has received the necessary instructions from Moscow.

02.56. MAYOR OF LENINGRAD'S PRESS CONFERENCE

LENINGRAD (RIA). After midnight, Leningrad's Mayor Anatoli Sobchak held a press conference at his office. In his opinion, the Aug. 19 coup will fail. "That is the agony of the communist regime," he believes.

Sobchak said that Col. Gen. Samsonov, commander of the Leningrad Military District, had given him an officer's word that troops would not be moved into the city. According to unconfirmed reports, however, there is some movement of army units towards Leningrad, after all. Tank columns are moving from the direction of Luga. Units of the Ryazan and Pskov airborne divisions are also heading for the city. According to some reports, a regiment of the Pskov Airborne Division is already stationed at the building of the regional KGB department and that of the Interior Ministry department of the Leningrad Region Executive Committee.

As for the regional department of the KGB, it must obey the directives of Russia's President, in the Mayor's opinion. At the same time Anatoli Sobchak did not rule out the possibility of the USSR KGB troops interfering in the events in the city.

02.57. ANATOLI SOBCHAK SUPPORTS CONVENING OF EMER-
GENCY CONGRESS
     LENINGRAD (RIA). At a press conference in the early hours of Aug. 20, Anatoli Sobchak said that he had had a telephone conversation with Boris Gidaspov, leader of the Leningrad communists. Gidaspov said that he did not have comprehensive information about the situation in the city, and believed that nothing unusual was happening in Leningrad. Leningrad's Mayor stated that earlier on Aug. 19 he had had a telephone conversation with Alexander Yakovlev, one of the leaders of the Movement for Democratic Reform, who had intended, one day before the coup, to distribute a letter to communists entitled "The Danger of a Revanchist Coup Grows with Every Hour".

According to Anatoli Sobchak, all the Deputies of the USSR supported the convocation of an emergency congress of the People's Deputies of the USSR. He also called on Leningraders gathered at Mariinsky Palace to go home. At the same time barricades were built at the Mayor's Office, and Molotov cocktails were prepared. OMON and Afghan war veterans set up a guard.

03.07. TVK INDEPENDENT TV COMPANY INFORMS INHABIT-
ANTS OF KAMCHATKA ABOUT EVENTS IN COUNTRY
     PETROPAVLOVSK-KAMCHATSKY (RIA). The information blockade of Kamchatka, organized by the State Emergency Committee, has been broken by the TVK independent Far Eastern TV company, which broadcasts early in the morning. Declaring its unconditional support for the government and President of Russia, it broadcasts live reports of its Moscow colleagues and of Kamchatka Deputies in the Russian parliament about events in the country.

Leaders of the local public organizations and parties under the umbrella movement of Democratic Russia have stated on TVK their condemnation of the anticonstitutional coup and their support for the Russian government. Representatives of the state mass media announced their readiness to provide comprehensive information to the regional channels of the Russian TV and radio. The democratically oriented paper Vesti, founded by the Regional Soviet of People's Deputies, put out a special issue devoted to the events of Aug. 19.

## 03.09. EDGAR SAVISAAR'S SPEECH ON ESTONIAN RADIO

TALLINN (RIA). At about one o'clock in the morning, Aug. 20, Edgar Savisaar, chairman of the government of Estonia, spoke on Estonian radio. He said that he did not believe in Mikhail Gorbachev's illness. In his view, the coup planners were trying to remove the USSR President from power in the crudest way.

Savisaar stressed that for the present it could not be said that the coup had succeeded, and that its organizers were holding all the levers of power. In the view of the head of the Estonian government, they had lost a great deal of time. The element of surprise had been essential for their success. At present, the putschists were forced to manoeuvre. Savisaar believed that a great deal would be decided in the next 24 hours, in which it would become clear who had seized the initiative.

The head of the Estonian government called on the republic's population not to carry out any decisions of the coup leaders.

## 03.11. MIKHAIL GORBACHEV HAS FLOWN FROM SIMFEROPOL: WHERE TO?

MOSCOW (RIA). According to unconfirmed reports received by an RIA reporter, USSR President Mikhail Gorbachev flew from Simferopol by plane late on Aug. 19. The ultimate destination of the flight was unknown. According to eyewitnesses, the President looked quite healthy.

## 03.16. ALEXANDER RUTSKOI APPEALS TO YOUNG PEOPLE

MOSCOW (RIA). Russian parliament radio broadcast an appeal from Alexander Rutskoi, Vice-President of Russia, to the young citizens of Russia. He called on everyone to make a choice which would determine the fate of Russia, stressed that no provocations or conflicts with the forces of the USSR Interior Ministry or the army should be permitted.

"Don't let yourselves be used in this dirty puppet war," he said. The resistance must be political; everything must be done to maintain law and order. He also expressed the conviction that in this tragic hour the young people would make the right choice in favour of freedom. Rutskoi also called on servicemen to obey the decree of Boris Yeltsin, President of Russia.

## 02.00. RIGA: HEADQUARTERS OF POPULAR FRONT OF LATVIA SEIZED

RIGA (RIA). According to sources in the Latvian parliament, about midnight Aug. 19 an unidentified military unit, supposedly the Riga Black Berets, seized the headquarters of the Popular Front of Latvia. Four activists who were on the premises were beaten up. One of them came to the Supreme Soviet of the republic to report the incident. According to his account, the attackers had come in a police van.

04.01. ARMY UNITS GUARD RUSSIA'S SUPREME SOVIET
    MOSCOW (RIA). According to RIA reporters on duty at the building
of the Russian parliament, a paratroop unit from Tula under Maj. Gen.
Lebed defending the Russian leadership's residency includes about 50
armoured vehicles. It has been reported that truckloads of paratroops armed
with assault rifles and grenade-launchers arrived there. They also mounted
guard at the White House. The troops and armoured vehicles surround the
whole of the building. Ivan Silayev, the Russian Prime Minister, inspected
the guards and pronounced himself satisfied with the way the troops were
organized.
    RIA has received unconfirmed reports that the Taman Motorized
Rifle Division, stationed near Moscow, had joined the Russian side.
According to the agency's reporters, about a hundred volunteer Muscovites
guarding the Russian parliament headed for the Moscow Soviet at about 3
in the morning to join the pickets there. In New Arbat, slabs of concrete were
moved into position to stop the passage of tanks to the Russian authorities'
residency.

04.50. SOVIET POWER ON PACIFIC COAST CALLS FOR SUPPORT
FOR YELTSIN
    VLADIVOSTOK (RIA). Sergei Solovyov, acting chairman of the
City Soviet, called on the population of Vladivostok not to obey the
directives of the unconstitutional State Emergency Committee.
    "All this is too much like a military coup," he said. "It is no accident
that it took place on the eve of the signing of the Union Treaty. Our readiness
to defend the achievements of perestroika, glasnost and democracy are now
tested."
    Solovyov told the citizens of his telephone conversation with Vladimir
Kuznetsov, chairman of the territorial executive committee, currently in
Moscow. Kuznetsov also called on his compatriots to obey the decrees of
the President of Russia.

04.52. TROOP MOVEMENTS IN LENINGRAD AREA
    LENINGRAD (RIA). About five in the morning, Aug. 20, a motor-
way patrol observed movement of an APC convoy along the Kiev motor-
way, some 52 km from Leningrad, heading for the city. According to
unconfirmed reports, two regiments of the Pskov Airborne Division are
already stationed in the city. The Emergency Committee's instructions from
Moscow were for all the units taking part in the seizure of power to move
into the city at midnight, but the order was not carried out.

04.57. CITY SOVIET OF PETROZAVODSK COMPLIES WITH DE-
CREES OF PRESIDENT OF RUSSIAN FEDERATION

PETROZAVODSK (RIA). Presidium of the Petrozavodsk City
Soviet passed a resolution on the political situation in the country.
It says that the local authorities accepted as guidelines for action the Aug. 19
decrees of the Russian President on the illegality of the State Emergency
Committee.

Beginning 8.00 a.m. on Aug. 20, the members of the presidium and
the deputies of the Petrozavodsk City Soviet will go to the city's enterprises
and organizations to explain and supervise the fulfilment of the Aug. 19
decrees of the President of Russia. The deputies intended to ask the workers
of the city's life support system to refrain from striking, choosing other
forms of political protest instead.

05.24. VITEBSK DIVISION OF USSR KGB APPROACHING LENIN-
GRAD

LENINGRAD (RIA). According to an RIA reporter, a convoy of the
USSR KGB Vitebsk Division, and of the Pskov Division of the USSR
Defence Ministry, is approaching Leningrad. Besides, 120 medium and 60
light tanks, and a battalion of APCs were observed heading for the city. At
five in the morning, Aug. 20, the column was sighted near Gatchina.

05.26. APPEAL OF DEMOCRATIC PARTY OF UKRAINE TO PRE-
SIDIUM OF REPUBLIC'S SUPREME SOVIET

KIEV (RIA). The presidium of the national council of the Democratic
Party of the Ukraine regards the removal from power of USSR President
Mikhail Gorbachev and the setting up of the State Emergency Committee
as an unconstitutional act and as a coup d'etat. The presidium called on the
Supreme Soviet of the Ukraine to resolutely distance itself from the plotters
and to take all the necessary measures for the defence of the Ukraine's state
sovereignty.

"We believe it necessary," states the appeal published here, "that the
Supreme Soviet of the Ukraine should declare all acts of the Emergency
Committee invalid on Ukrainian territory, and stipulate criminal responsibility of officials for carrying out the decrees of the putschists' self-
appointed committee."

06.07. IVAN SILAYEV APPEALS TO NIGHT PICKETS

MOSCOW (RIA). Early in the morning of Aug. 20 Russian Prime
Minister Ivan Silayev spoke on the Russian parliament's radio. He thanked
everyone who took part in the night vigil round the parliament building, and
declared that the picket would be regarded as a full working day with double
pay. The Russian Premier asked the night pickets to stay until nine or ten
o'clock in the morning, until fresh forces arrived on the scene.

## 06.09. KAMCHATKA AUTHORITIES DENY REPORT ON STATE EMERGENCY COMMITTEE BEING SET UP

PETROPAVLOVSK-KAMCHATSKY (RIA). The presidium of the Kamchatka Regional Soviet denied press reports about alleged setting-up of an emergency committee on the peninsula. The local authorities' appeal to the population states their solidarity with the position of the Russian President and the leadership of Russia. Legally elected organs of power and the Constitution of the Russian Federation are in force on the region's territory.

Chairman of the Soviet Pyotr Premyak told an RIA correspondent that the local departments of the KGB and of the Interior Ministry declared their readiness to obey unconditionally the directives of the Soviet. Head of the military garrison of Petropavlovsk-Kamchatsky expressed loyalty to the Soviet. Jointly with its newspaper, Vesti, the Kamchatka Soviet organized the printing and distribution of the decrees of President Boris Yeltsin. The local coordinating council of the Democratic Russia movement voiced its support to the actions of the legally elected organs of power.

The situation on Kamchatka is normal. All holders of public offices have been warned that compliance with the directives of the State Emergency Committee is illegal.

## 06.54. CITY POPULATION'S RALLY TO BE HELD IN MOSCOW AT PARLIAMENT BUILDING

MOSCOW (RIA). The citizens' rally against the introduction of the state of emergency in the USSR, planned for 12 o'clock in Manege Square, will be held in front of the Russian parliament building. This was reported early in the morning on Aug. 20 by the "White House Radio". The reason for the change in the venue of this mass action, sanctioned by the Acting Mayor of Moscow Yuri Luzhkov, is that the Russian leadership has information that the rally will be dispersed by the military using tear-gas.

## 06.58. FAR EAST: WAR ON AIR

KHABAROVSK (RIA). On Aug. 20, the only independent radio station in the region, Far East--Russia, was silent. According to telephone message No. 4/182 signed by Titov, head of the territory's state radio broadcast centre, its transmitters are decommissioned. Previously they had been used to jam foreign radio stations.

In the meantime, a powerful unidentified radio station unexpectedly started broadcasting in Khabarovsk. Despite attempts to jam it, it broadcast the texts of the Russian government's statements.

## 07.03. FOREIGNERS LEAVE FAR EAST

KHABAROVSK (RIA). On Aug. 20, foreign tourists and business-men were observed leaving the Khabarovsk Intourist hotel en masse. They hurried to leave the area by plane and train via Nakhodka. Previously planned meetings and negotiations with foreign enterprises are cancelled. Several Japanese delegations telexed their refusal to come to Khabarovsk "on account of the unstable situation in the USSR."

## 07.05. KHABAROVSK TRADE UNIONS DO NOT RECOGNIZE STATE EMERGENCY COMMITTEE

KHABAROVSK (RIA). The trade union committee of the Khabarovsk Daldiesel Plant passed a resolution recognizing the State Emergency Committee as illegal, and declared that it obeyed the legally elected President of Russia and the government of the republic. The workers demanded that USSR President Mikhail Gorbachev, removed from his post on Aug. 19 by the plotters, appear on national TV. Similar decisions were passed at other plants of Khabarovsk as well.

## 07.44. CITY SOVIET OF VLADIVOSTOK CALLS ON STATE EMER-GENCY COMMITTEE TO GIVE THEMSELVES UP TO LEGALLY ELECTED AUTHORITY

VLADIVOSTOK (RIA). On Aug. 21, Sergei Solovyov, acting chairman of the City Soviet, spoke on the local radio. He said that City Soviet Deputies had gone to work collectives and military units to explain to the people the meaning of the appeal of Russian President Boris Yeltsin to the citizens of Russia. An emergency session of the City Soviet was appointed for 16.00 local time. A draft resolution of the session calls on the members of the State Emergency Committee to give themselves up to the legally elected powers.

The situation in the territory is normal, said Solovyov. The territorial department of the KGB is working as usual. The units of the Pacific Ocean Fleet and of the border troops do nothing to aggravate the situation, although the number of joint police and military patrol units has been increased from 30 to 40.

## 07.54. DIRECTIVE OF GOVERNMENT OF MOLDOVA

MOLDOVA (RIA). To prevent the spread of misinformation and of materials of unconstitutional nature which may lead to aggravation of the socio-political situation in the republic it is deemed necessary:

(1) to ban, until further notice, the publication on the territory of the Republic of Moldova of the following newspapers: Trud, Rabochaya tribuna, Izvestia, Pravda, Krasnaya zvezda, Sovetskaya Rossiya, Moskovskaya pravda, Selskaya zhizn;

(2) to warn editors of republican, district and city newspapers that in case of publication in their papers of materials promulgated by the State Emergency Committee the papers in question will be banned;

(3) the ban on the papers listed in point (1) will be lifted by a special directive from the government of the Republic of Moldova.

Valeriu Muravsky,

Primer Minister of the Republic of Moldova

## 07.58. FORTY ENTERPRISES OF KRASNODAR TERRITORY IN-TEND TO PARTICIPATE IN STRIKE

KRASNODAR (RIA). According to information received by an RIA correspondent at the Supreme Soviet of the Russian Federation, more than 40 enterprises of Krasnodar Territory are ready to go on strike on Aug. 20. They include the Feigin Machine-Building Plant and the Cotton Combine. The strike is intended to begin at 9.00 a.m. local time. The cities of Maikop, Novorossiisk and Sochi are expected to be the major centres of the political strike. In Krasnodar, a rally of protest against the coup will gather at noon near the executive committee building. The position of the territorial executive committee is not clear. On instructions from the committee on glasnost of the territorial Soviet of People's Deputies, only information coming over the radio is published. A meeting has been appointed for 9.00 a.m. of democratically minded deputies of the Russian Federation. At noon, these deputies intend to fly to Moscow.

## 08.02. AIRBORNE TROOPS COMMANDER UNDER ARREST

MOSCOW (RIA). According to information received by an RIA correspondent from informed sources, Lt. Gen. Pavel Grachev, com-mander-in-chief of airborne troops of the USSR Ministry of Defence, was arrested on Aug. 19. It became clear from a conversation with a highly placed official from the Russian leadership that the paratroop unit which had arrived from Tula to defend the Russian parliament building was carrying out orders from Grachev.

## 08.08. TROOP MOVEMENTS IN VLADIVOSTOK

VLADIVOSTOK (RIA). Late on Aug. 19 and early on Aug. 20, movements of convoys of tanks and APCs were observed on the approaches to Vladivostok from Gornostai Bay. Col. Yuri Zelensky, military comman-dant of the Vladivostok garrison, explained to an RIA correspondent that the movements of the armoured vehicles were connected with the plans for the battle training of the units stationed in the city. ''The army carries out its constitutional duty,'' he said.

## 08.14. PROTEST RALLIES IN VLADIVOSTOK

VLADIVOSTOK (RIA). ''We are indignant at the actions of the State Emergency Committee which has mounted an illegal attempt to seize power in the country,'' an RIA correspondent was told at the trade union committee of the Vladivostok porcelain factory. ''The workers fully support Russian President Boris Yeltsin's appeal to the people, and the call for a political strike.''

Protest rallies against the anticonstitutional plot intended to overthrow the country's legally elected leadership were held on Aug. 20 by the workers of the May First Ship Repair Works and the Vladivostok merchant navy port.

## 08.17. SPECIAL BODIES SET UP IN PRIMORYE TERRITORY IN CONNECTION WITH STATE OF EMERGENCY

VLADIVOSTOK (RIA). Russian Deputy Alexei Volyntsev, chairman of the territorial Soviet, announced on local radio on Aug. 20 the setting up in the Primorye territory of a coordinating commission in connection with the declaration of the state of emergency; a special consultative committee attached to the territorial Soviet has also been appointed. The latter includes representatives of local administration, Pacific Fleet command, and managers of industrial enterprises. Volyntsev called on the population of the territory to remain calm and exercise restraint, not to be carried away by emotion, and to continue work at their workplaces.

## 09.31. LENINGRAD: DECISION OF THE RUSSIAN FEDERATION SUPREME SOVIET SESSION AWAITED

LENINGRAD (RIA). According to information received by RIA, Vice-Mayor Vyacheslav Scherbakov, Chairman of the Leningrad Soviet Alexander Belyayev, and People's Deputy Marina Salye decided, at a meeting of the headquarters for the liquidation of the consequences of the coup d'etat, to call on all Leningrad enterprises to continue work as usual until a decision is taken by the Russian parliament.

At Leningrad underground stations people listen to broadcasts of the decrees and directives of the President of Russia and of the Supreme Soviet of the Russian Federation, as well as decisions and directives of the Leningrad Soviet and Mayor. Military censorship has been introduced at the Leningrad radio station. According to Vice-Mayor Vyacheslav Scherbakov, the city is surrounded by a tight circle of troops. However, convoys of troops that were moving towards Leningrad from Luga have stopped and turned into side roads some 70 kilometres from the city. The newspapers Smena and Nevskoye vremya published early on Aug. 20 were distributed through alternative channels, not the official Soyuzpechat.

A rally is at present in progress at the Kirov Works production association.

10.36. RUSSIAN PRESIDENT'S APPEAL TO CHAIRMAN OF USSR SUPREME SOVIET

MOSCOW (RIA). Russian President Boris Yeltsin sent the following letter to Anatoli Lukyanov, Chairman of the USSR Supreme Soviet:

"In view of unconstitutional acts by a group of persons styling themselves 'the Soviet leadership' we believe it necessary to undertake the following:

"(1) to organize within 24 hours since your receipt of the present document a meeting between Boris Yeltsin, Ivan Silayev, Ruslan Khasbulatov, and USSR President Mikhail Gorbachev; to invite Gennadi Yanayev to the meeting;

"(2) to conduct in the nearest three days a medical examination of President Gorbachev by expert specialists of the World Health Organization; the Russian government will assume the funding of the expense in hard currency;

"(3) to publish the results of the examination; in case the result of the examination is positive, conditions must immediately be created for the USSR President to resume his duties;

"(4) to lift all restrictions on the work of the Russian mass media, the more so that no such restrictions were imposed on mass media in the other republics;

"(5) to lift the state of emergency throughout the entire territory of the Russian Federation during the session of the RSFSR Supreme Soviet, and to ensure safe travel and arrival to Moscow of the Russian Deputies;

"(6) to withdraw the troops to their permanent locations;

"(7) to ensure unhindered functioning of the President of the Russian Federation in his residency in the Kremlin;

"(8) to restore the operation of all types of communications necessary for the normal functioning of the Russian administration;

"(9) to stop all threats to the Russian leadership and to ensure its immunity and freedom of movement.

"(10) to announce the dissolution of the illegally formed State Emergency Committee in the USSR, and to cancel all its directives and orders.

*Boris Yeltsin, President of the Russian Federation*
*Alexander Rutskoi, Vice-President*
*Ivan Silayev, Chairman of the RSFSR Council of Ministers*
*Ruslan Khasbulatov, Acting Chairman of the RSFSR Supreme Soviet."*

10.40. VOLOGDA POPULATION IN FAVOUR OF LAW AND ORDER

VOLOGDA (RIA). The chairmen of the regional Soviet and executive committee have passed a resolution calling on the population of the region to continue the harvest. People's Deputies of the USSR and Russia

from the Vologda Region sent telegrams to the Supreme Soviets of the
USSR and the Russian Federation demanding the convocation of emergency congresses.

The journalists of the newspaper Russky Sever have polled the
population in the streets of the regional centre. So far, the people have too
little information to form definite judgements on the events, but most
support the "tendency towards law and order".

**10.41. ANNOUNCEMENT OF THE RUSSIAN FEDERATION SUPREME SOVIET PRESIDIUM'S PRESS SERVICE**
MOSCOW (RIA). A briefing for the foreign press will be held today,
Aug. 20, in the Russian parliament building at 11.30 a.m., room 3-50.
Entrance through door No. 8. Access permitted to holders of any accreditation documents for the foreign press.

**10.45. PETROZAVODSK SOCIAL-DEMOCRATS CALL RALLY IN SUPPORT OF RUSSIAN AUTHORITIES**
PETROZAVODSK (RIA). As an RIA reporter learned at the spontaneously organized headquarters in support of the Russian leadership set up
at the local division of the Social Democratic Party of Russia, Col. Toropov
of the Interior Ministry of the Karelian Republic suggested that they put in
an official request for permission to hold a rally in order to avoid undesirable
excesses. The rally is appointed for 18.00, Aug. 20. On Aug. 19, the
headquarters received from the Russian parliament all official documents
signed by the Russian leaders, and distributed them at the city's enterprises.
The working people expressed support for the Russian leadership, but there
was no question of going on strike so far.

**10.48. PEOPLE'S DEPUTIES GO TO MILITARY UNITS**
MOSCOW (RIA). A group of Deputies of Russia, including Father
Gleb Yakunin, Bella Denisenko, Victor Aksyuchits, Victor Sheinis, Mikhail
Astafyev, Yuri Yeltsov and others, went to the units of the Moscow
garrison. The deputies intend to inform the servicemen of the situation in the
country in connection with the latest events, and of the positions and actions
of the Russian leadership.

**10.53. KRASNODAR: SITUATION TENSE**
KRASNODAR (RIA). On the night of Aug. 19/20, activists of the
Democratic Russia movement managed to print the Decree of the President
of the Russian Federation and his appeal to the Russians. These documents
are pasted up at factory gates and trolleybuses, and are handed out in the
streets. On Aug. 20, Komsomolets Kubani, the only paper to publish these
documents on the first page, appeared. According to information from the

City Soviet, Vladimir Gorshkov, chairman of the executive committee's commission on glasnost, tried to prevent these publications, declaring that the only information to be published must come from TASS. The situation in the city is tense.

WASHINGTON (PF). George Bush's press conference. Question: Do you have any plans to discontinue the process of economic cooperation developing in the last few months.? Answer: I believe that the process will be suspended. To support democracy, to support reform, not only the United States but Europe as well will suspend everything. A great deal is at stake in all this. Naturally I shall not continue aid or assistance if I run into such unconstitutional acts carried out by a handful of people backed by the military.

WASHINGTON (PF). Citing statements by highly placed representatives of the administration who refused permission to mention their names, AP lists the following measures now being considered: refusal to support the USSR's associated membership in the World Bank and the International Monetary Fund; refusal to offer the USSR the most favoured nation status in trade; putting off the departure of the new American Ambassador to the USSR Robert Strauss for Moscow; the demand for Moscow to call back the USSR's Ambassador to the United States, Victor Komplektov; re-imposition of a number of recently lifted restrictions on the sale to the USSR of computers and other high-tech equipment. AP stresses that the administration is not unanimous on the issue of the measures to be taken, and that some members of the administration believe that the imposition of such restrictions may undermine reform in the USSR.

## 11.15. TYUMEN NOT ON STRIKE SO FAR

TYUMEN (RIA). Tyumen's oil-industry workers have not so far gone on strike, although this option is still considered. Supporting Russian President Boris Yeltsin, the presidium of the Regional Soviet of People's Deputies issued a recommendation not to make hasty decisions on strike action, partly for technological reasons. Once stopped, an oil rig is very hard to start again, Nikolai Tikhonov, chairman of the regional trade union committee told an RIA correspondent over the telephone.

## 11.22. A MEETING BETWEEN RUSSIAN LEADERSHIP AND LUKYA-NOV HELD IN KREMLIN

MOSCOW (RIA). It was announced in the Russian parliament building today that a meeting is at present in progress between Russian Vice-President Alexander Rutskoi, Acting Chairman of the Russian Federation Supreme Soviet Ruslan Khasbulatov and Russia's Prime Minister Ivan Silayev, and Anatoli Lukyanov, Chairman of the USSR Supreme Soviet. Russian statesmen brought an appeal from the Russian President to the Chairman of the USSR Supreme Soviet outlining the Russian leadership's demands for normalizing the situation.

Gennadi Burbulis, Russian Federation State Secretary, told Russian Deputies that Lukyanov suggested in a telephone conversation that the latest events had been completely unexpected by him and that he was at the time on leave.

## 11.31. ANNOUNCEMENT OF RUSSIAN FEDERATION SUPREME SOVIET PRESIDIUM'S PRESS SERVICE

MOSCOW (RIA). Presidium of the Russian Federation Supreme Soviet has passed a resolution to convene an emergency session of the Russian Federation Supreme Soviet on Aug. 21, at 11.00 a.m. in the Russian parliament building (2, Krasnopresnenskaya Embankment).

Members of Soviet and foreign mass media holding previously valid accreditation documents will be permitted to attend the fourth session of the Russian Federation Supreme Soviet. Information available at telephone No. 205-98-03.

LONDON (PF). Late Monday, Britain's Prime Minister John Major made a statement to journalists on the events in the USSR. ''What we saw in the USSR is an outright old-fashioned coup,'' he said. ''I believe a number of issues will be raised at a meeting of foreign ministers of the EC countries. In particular, the issue of early agreements on cooperation between the EC and such countries as Poland, Hungary and Czechoslovakia.''

Douglas Hurd, Britain's Secretary of State for Foreign and Commonwealth Affairs, announced on Monday the suspension of the 50 million pound government programme initiated two months ago to help the USSR train managerial personnel.

PARIS (PF). French President Francois Mitterrand demanded that Soviet leaders guarantee the life and freedom of Mikhail Gorbachev and Boris Yeltsin.

Citing French Foreign Minister Roland Dumas, the France Press agency reported from the Hague that France demanded the return to power of USSR President Mikhail Gorbachev, at a meeting of foreign ministers of the 12 countries of the European Community held in Netherlands.

## 11.54. MIKHAIL GORBACHEV POSSIBLY NEAR MOSCOW

MOSCOW (RIA). According to reports reaching RIA, Mikhail Gorbachev was brought tonight to Moscow by plane. The plane carrying the President touched down at a military airfield at Chkalovsk (30 kilometres north-east of Moscow). At the present moment, the President of the USSR is guarded at one of his residencies near Moscow by KGB troops. According to unconfirmed reports, Air Force Col. Gen. Yevgeni Shaposhnikov, Commander-in-Chief of the USSR Air Force, is under arrest.

## 11.57. ARREST OF RUSSIAN DEPUTY

MOSCOW (RIA). At midnight, Russian Deputy Mikhail Kamchatov was arrested near his home. According to his wife, Kamchatov was arrested by security agents, and taken to an army unit. He was allowed to telephone his family.

## 12.00. RADIO STATIONS SET UP AT RUSSIAN PARLIAMENT BUILDING

MOSCOW (RIA). Russian State Secretary Gennadi Burbulis said that during the past night four radio stations have been set up in the parliament building; they broadcast in short and medium wave metre bands. Russian Deputies, deprived of the ordinary means of mass communication, can only rely on these radio stations and foreign Russian-language radio services.

## 12.07. RALLY AT RUSSIAN PARLIAMENT BUILDING BEGUN

MOSCOW (RIA). At noon, a rally of the capital's citizens began at the parliament building; it was sanctioned by Moscow's Vice-Mayor Yuri Luzhkov and organized by the Democratic Russia movement and councils of work collectives of Moscow and the Moscow Region. Eduard Shevardnadze and Alexander Yakovlev, leaders of the Movement for Democratic Reform, are expected to take part in it. The rally's slogan is "In defence of law and order".

Several dozens of thousands of people have gathered for the rally. In the last few minutes, the situation at the Russian parliament building has deteriorated after paratroop units guarding it during the night left.

## 12.17. DECREE REMOVING YELTSIN FROM POWER IN PREPARATION

MOSCOW (RIA). Sergei Shakhrai, chairman of the parliamentary legislation committee, announced at a general meeting of People's Deputies that, according to unconfirmed reports, the State Emergency Committee is preparing a decree removing Russian President Yeltsin from power and instituting criminal proceedings against him; a similar move is aimed against Konstantin Kobets, chairman of the Russian Federation State Committee for Defence. This committee informed an RIA correspondent that in Krasnoyarsk a rally in Interior Ministry units in support of Yeltsin is in its seventh hour.

## 12.21. STRIKES IN VORKUTA AND SEVEROURALSK

MOSCOW (RIA). Yuri Kovalenko, member of Vorkuta's workers' committee, confirmed in a telephone conversation with an RIA correspondent that miners of the Vorkuta coalfield have gone on a political strike. By

13.00 on Aug. 20, the five mines already on strike must be joined by others. According to the executive committee of the Independent Miners Union, bauxite mine, a mine-building trust and a furniture factory are on strike in Severouralsk. The strikers include 3.5 thousand men working underground.

## 12.24 KRASNODAR: DEMOCRATIC PARTY OF RUSSIA ORGAN-IZED RALLY

KRASNODAR (RIA). Hundreds gathered for a rally called by the Democratic Party of Russia in the centre of Krasnodar, held under the slogan, "Prosecute the Communist Junta!" At present, the Democratic Party of Russia informs the population of the decrees of Russian President Boris Yeltsin. The police treats the demonstrators without hostility; the situation is quiet.

## 12.30. MILITARY IN LENINGRAD TAKE POSITIVE ATTITUDE TO YELTSIN'S APPEAL

LENINGRAD (RIA). Col. Ivan Ivanov, head of the operations group of the State Emergency Committee for the Leningrad Military District, told an RIA correspondent that "all the units of the Leningrad military district are in their permanent quarters; the troops, including units used to maintain public order, make no movements at all."

Asked about the attitude of the servicemen of the district towards the appeal of Boris Yeltsin and the Leningrad Soviet, he replied, "Positive." Police Col. Sergei Kuznetsov, deputy head of the Leningrad public security service, said that he knew of no troop movements.

At a rally in Palace Square on Aug. 19, Anatoli Sobchak stated that by agreement with the commander of the Leningrad Military District, the troops heading towards Leningrad had been stopped some 70 kilometres from the city.

TOKYO (PF). Prime Minister Toshiki Kaifu said that the night before he had had emergency telephone consultations with US President George Bush and Canada's Prime Minister Brian Mulroney. "A unanimous opinion has been expressed that no sliding back must be allowed in the present situation," said Kaifu, stressing that the G-7 countries at the last summit in London had committed themselves to a "true course of perestroika" in the Soviet Union.

OTTAWA (PF). Canada's Prime Minister Brian Mulroney stated that Ottawa did not recognize the new Soviet leadership, and that all aid to the Soviet Union would be discontinued until assurances were received on the continuation of reform and safety of Mikhail Gorbachev and his family.

MADRID (PF). Felipe Gonzalez stated that credits to the tune of 150 thousand million pesetas offered to the Soviet Union would be frozen if the plot in that country was confirmed.

BELGRADE (PF). The TANYUG agency distributed an official report on the results of the meeting which says that "the coup in the USSR was carried out by conservative elements relying on the Soviet Army and the KGB, and has major international repercussions; it will also affect the situation in Yugoslavia. There is no doubt that there is a real danger of the repetition of such a scenario in Yugoslavia."

## 12.34. APPEAL OF PRESIDIUM OF MOSCOW SOVIET TO MILITARY

MOSCOW (RIA). Presidium of the Moscow Soviet has issued the following appeal to all soldiers, sergeants, ensigns, officers and generals: "Brothers! The old upper crust of the party is making a last desperate attempt to retain its power and privileges at any cost. Those who led luxurious lives at the expense of the poverty of the people in their stately homes and dachas are again preparing a bloodbath for those who struggle for the right to land, for the right to live as befits human beings. Mikhail Gorbachev, the legally elected President of the USSR, has been removed from power. An attempt is made to remove from power Boris Yeltsin, the President of the Russian Federation elected by the whole people. They are planning to fool you again, as they fooled you in Afghanistan, only this time they want to make you shoot at your own people. Do not start a civil war, do not open fire, do not become executioners of your own people. Each of you will have to answer before God and the people for his actions today."

## 12.36. MINERS' STRIKES SPREADING

MOSCOW (RIA). An RIA corespondent was told at the Independent Miners Union that by early Aug. 20, miners of the Vorkuta and North-Urals coalfields stopped work. Forty per cent of the mines in the Kemerovo Region are on strike.

The trade unions are conducting negotiations with the miners of Yakutia and railwaymen in an attempt to get their commitment to strike.

## 12.56. PSKOV: LAW ENFORCEMENT INSTITUTIONS TAKE WAIT-AND-SEE ATTITUDE

PSKOV (RIA). Anatoli Kartunov, chairman of the Pskov department of the KGB, linked his attitude towards the State Emergency Committee with the results of the coming session of the USSR Supreme Soviet. He told an RIA correspondent that his unit was taking a wait-and-see attitude.

Asked by RIA whether he had any information about a certain salvation committee organized at the CPSU regional committee, the region's public prosecutor Valentin Komsyukov replied negatively. At the present movement, he saw fighting all violations of law as his main task. Pavel Pushnitsky, acting head of the city police department, said that the police units were obeying his orders. The main task of the men of the city department of the Interior Ministry, as defined by Pushnitsky, was enforcing law and order in the streets, and combating crime.

13.08. CALL FOR CALM TO POPULATION OF KAMCHATKA

PETROPAVLOVSK-KAMCHATSKY (RIA). A joint appeal to the population and military of Kamchatka has been adopted at a meeting of the presidium and executive committee of the Kamchatka Regional Soviet, heads of enterprises and organizations, Kamchatka's trade union federation and the commanding officers of the garrison. The declaration says that no state of emergency has been imposed on the peninsula, and that legally elected authorities are in power. It is stressed that all the necessary measures will be taken immediately in case of provocative actions devitalizing the situation. The authors of the appeal call on the population of Kamchatka to be reasonable and calm, not to succumb to panic, and to show solidarity in the interests of the country.

13.13. LITHUANIA READY FOR POLITICAL STRIKE

VILNIUS (RIA). Expressing solidarity with the democratic forces of Russia, the Supreme Soviet of the Lithuanian Republic has decided, in case the parliament and the government of the Lithuanian Republic can no longer fulfil their duties, to call on the population of Lithuania to begin an indefinite political strike, reports Elta agency. If the Supreme Soviet and government are able to carry out their duties, the population of Lithuania will support democratic Russia through manifestations and meetings at their workplaces. WARSAW (PF). Representative of the Polish government for the press, minister Andzej Zarembski outlined the Polish government's position on the situation in the USSR. The Polish government monitors the events in the USSR with close attention. We regard the situation after the imposition of the state of emergency as serious. Its consequences for Poland are now analyzed. We are profoundly convinced that the course of history cannot be turned back by force. We see proof of this in the Polish experience of martial law, and in the principal idea of Solidarity: even the most difficult problems should be solved through dialogue, not violence.

WASHINGTON (PF). Reuters reports from Washington: the Federation of American Scientists announced on Monday that it would declare ''scientific boycott'' against the Soviet Union if its present leaders refuse Mikhail Gorbachev a chance to speak out freely.

13.31. MOSCOW REGIONAL SOVIET FORMED COORDINATING COMMITTEE IN SUPPORT OF RUSSIAN GOVERNMENT

MOSCOW (RIA). On Aug. 20, Moscow Regional Soviet formed a committee for coordinating the activities of Soviets on the territory of the

Moscow Region, for links with the Moscow City Soviet and the government of Russia.

Late on Aug. 19, the presidium of the Moscow Regional Soviet decided to obey the directives of the Russian government. Of the 16 members of the presidium, only its chairman, Ivan Cherepanov, abstained, while the rest voted for the motion.

The committee's first move was to distribute the decrees and resolutions of the Russian government throughout the regional towns in the Moscow Region by telephone and messengers.

13.40. ALEXANDER RUTSKOI ON THE MEETING WITH ANATOLI LUKYANOV

MOSCOW (RIA). The conversation of representatives of the Russian leadership with Anatoli Lukyanov, Chairman of the USSR Supreme Soviet, "was tense at first, but then the discussion centred on each point and each position," said Vice-President Alexander Rutskoi. In a conversation with journalists, Rutskoi informed them of the meeting with the head of the Soviet parliament on Aug. 20, attended also by Ruslan Khasbulatov and Ivan Silayev.

"Lukyanov agrees that some points in the Emergency Committee's documents do not agree with the laws of the USSR. He will therefore convoke today the Presidium of the Supreme Soviet of the country, and all these documents will be considered," he said.

"I shall insist on Gorbachev's presence at this sitting," Lukyanov said, according to Rutskoi. The Chairman of the Supreme Soviet of the USSR counts on a phone conversation with Mikhail Gorbachev today. As far as he knows, he "is alive and well, but there have been certain setbacks to his health--high blood pressure and lumbago, they say." Rutskoi said that at present the President of the USSR is in the Crimea.

According to the latest information received by RIA from confidential sources, USSR President Mikhail Gorbachev is still at his dacha in the Crimea, guarded by a special unit of KGB troops. This unit "cannot guarantee the President's life" in case of any attempt to free the President by force, says our source.

13.47. NAKHODKA'S DEPUTIES GO ON POLITICAL STRIKE

NAKHODKA (RIA). Deputies of the Nakhodka City Soviet at a session held Aug. 20 declared members of the Emergency Committee who have removed the legally elected President of the country, Mikhail Gorbachev, from power to be a "group of impostors, a junta, and traitors". A decision was passed unanimously to obey Russian laws only. The deputies declared that they began a political strike to be expressed in gathering signatures to back the demand for removing the members of the Emergency Committee from power and instituting legal proceedings against them. It was decided to refrain from an economic strike, for the life support of tankers, fishing vessels and technical ships now at sea depended on the work of the enterprises.

TRIPOLI (PF). JANA agency reports that on Monday the leader of the Libyan revolution Muammar Gaddafi sent a telegram to Gennadi Yanayev. What follows is the text of that telegram: "To President Gennadi Yanayev, chairman of the State Emergency Committee in the USSR. We are happy to congratulate you on your bold historical act. We hope that it will lead the USSR from the deadly crisis in which it was plunged by a large-scale imperialist plot aimed not only against the Soviet Union but also against all peoples of the world. We resolutely support your act, for a united Soviet Union as a second world force is vitally necessary for peace in the whole world which is everywhere threatened because at present only one, barbaric force is active. The forces hostile to freedom, peace and progress can only be contained by force, as they do not know any moral and ethical values. Historically, the USSR is a factor of containment of colonialism and imperialism. Your great deed is supported by all the peoples of the Third World subjected against their will to violence and disunion as a result of the perfidious intentions of imperialism. This deed is very important for the revival of the world prestige of the USSR, of the dignity of the Soviet citizen which the imperialists wanted to trample under their dirty feet, and also for restoring the unity so needed by the peoples and territories of the USSR. We confirm the adherence of the Socialist People's Libyan Arab Jamahiriya to firm historical friendship with the USSR, which we did not forgo under any conditions. Libya is in favour of the cause of peace, socialism and freedom of all the peoples and their principles--unlike the wavering, weak and greedy. We confirm that we support you and stand at your side. Long live revolutionary struggle in the name of freedom, socialism and peace."

13.53. APPEAL OF COMMITTEE OF SOLDIERS' MOTHERS

MOSCOW (RIA). On Aug. 20, the Committee of Soldiers' Mothers called on all soldiers and seamen not to allow themselves to be turned into murderers rand not to carry out criminal orders. The appeal says that the parliamentary path of reforms in the Soviet Union has been blocked. It is the fault of all mothers and fathers, of all citizens, that the coup was carried out. The Committee of Soldiers' Mothers stressed that the troops were thrown into the streets against their will to intimidate the people, and called on the population not to insult them or provoke conflicts.

14.01. ALL-UNION PUBLIC OPINION CENTRE: KRASNOYARSK CITIZENS DO NOT SUPPORT EMERGENCY COMMITTEE OR EXPECT ANY GOOD FROM IT

MOSCOW (RIA). 76 per cent of the 266 citizens of Krasnoyarsk questioned by the All-Union Public Opinion Centre on Aug. 20, "Do you believe the activities of the State Emergency Committee to be legal?" gave a negative answer. Twelve per cent gave a positive answer; the same number found it difficult to reply at all.

The question, "Will the coming to power of the State Emergency Committee lead to deterioration or improvement of the economic situation in the country?" was answered like this: "The economy will deteriorate", 77 per cent; "The economy will improve," 9 per cent; 14 per cent gave no answer at all.

Sixty-one per cent of those polled believe that mass repressions will begin; 23 per cent do not agree with this view; 16 per cent have no opinion. Boris Yeltsin's call for an indefinite strike was supported by 57 per cent of the respondents, 33 per cent spoke out against it, nine per cent found it difficult to answer the question.

TALLINN (PF). The Estonian republican council of strike committees supported the activities of the State Emergency Committee aimed at restoring the Constitution of the USSR and the laws of the USSR on the territory of the Soviet Union. The government of the Estonian Republic has learnt that the heads of the industrial enterprises administered from the centre sent telegrams to the State Emergency Committee demanding that the mass media of the Estonian Republic be taken under military control.

14.39. CENTRAL COMMITTEE OF COMMUNIST PARTY DISCUSSED POSSIBILITY OF CONVENING PLENUM

MOSCOW (RIA). RIA has learned that CPSU Central Committee members held a debate today on convening an emergency plenary session of the Central Committee of the CPSU intended to relieve Mikhail Gorbachev of his duties as General Secretary of the CPSU. One of the participants in the debate said that the initiators of convening the session found themselves in the minority.

14.50. BELOZERTSEV AND KALUGIN THREATENED WITH ARREST

MOSCOW (RIA). According to RIA from confidential sources, members of the State Emergency Committee, Head of the KGB Vladimir Kryuchkov and Minister of the Interior Boris Pugo, gave the order for the arrest of People's Deputies Sergei Belozertsev and Oleg Kalugin. It is suggested that these deputies could try to hide in a foreign embassy. It is not discounted, that in the event of their detention, Kalugin is threatened with physical destruction and Belozertsev with internment.

### 15.01. IOJ PROTESTS AGAINST CENSORSHIP IN THE USSR

PRAGUE (RIA). The international organization of journalists (IOJ) has issued a statement expressing concern at the latest events in the USSR. It calls upon Soviet journalists to resist censorship and to seek all possible means of carrying out their professional duty--to truthfully inform the public. The address was signed by president of the IOJ Armando Rollenburg and its General Secretary Gerard Gatino.

### 15.05. PRESIDENT'S ADVISER DOES NOT INTEND TO RETURN TO MOSCOW

MOSCOW (RIA). According to RIA, from a reliable source, the USSR President's adviser Vitali Ignatenko has been on vacation in a private sanatorium in Sochi. "Ignatenko is not interested in the situation, he has not called to his office and does not intend to return," RIA was told.

### 15.09. RSFSR FOREIGN MINISTRY NOTE

MOSCOW (RIA). On Aug. 20, the Russian Foreign Ministry disseminated a note containing the following: "On the night of August 18-19, 1991, the legally elected President of the country was removed from power. In accordance with Russian President Yeltsin's Decree and Resolution No. 435 of 19 August 1991, all decisions made in the name of or on the orders of the so-called State Emergency Committee are considered illegal and invalid on the territory of the Russian Federation. In accordance with the foregoing, the RSFSR Foreign Ministry representative is authorized to declare: The Russian Government rejects responsibility for any actions taken or obligations assumed by the so-called State Emergency Committee, or on its orders, and requests that all countries and states of the world take measures to freeze all gold and currency reserves, as well as cargo, belonging to the USSR until an extraordinary Congress of People's Deputies of the USSR is called."

### 15.17. APPEAL TO SOVIET SERVICEMEN STATIONED IN LITHUANIA

VILNIUS (RIA). The Supreme Soviet of Lithuania appealed to soldiers and officers of the USSR armed forces stationed in Lithuania not to infringe upon the lives of population of Lithuania and the democratically elected leadership of the republic and state structures.

The Supreme Soviet of Lithuania hopes that soldiers are aware of Boris Yeltsin's Decree in which the activities of the State Emergency Committee are regarded as a state crime.

15.26. THE CPSU CENTRAL COMMITTEE IS PREPARING TO DE-
STROY OFFICIAL DOCUMENTS

MOSCOW (RIA). As one of the CPSU Central Committee officials
said RIA today, workers of the CC International Department were ordered
to prepare for destruction of secret documents and material for official use.
This source could not say whether or not other departments of the Central
Committee had received similar orders.

KIEV (PF). The organizational committee of the Socialist Union of
Ukrainian Students welcomes and supports the efforts of the State Emergency Committee to stabilize Soviet society. Chairman of the Organizational Committee Vladislav Buger. Kiev 252101, 37 Ul. Lomonosova,
Hostel 2. Room 56/2.

15.39. FISHERMEN IN VLADIVOSTOK HAVE BEGUN A POLITICAL
STRIKE

VLADIVOSTOK (RIA). At a meeting held on Aug. 20, workers of
the Pacific Administration of Reconnaissance Scientific Research Fleet
supported unanimously the decrees of Russian President Boris Yeltsin. The
trade union committee called a political strike. All life supporting fleet
systems will continue to operate but vessels will not leave their moorings.
It has been decided not to unload produce ordered by the state so that
supplies to the Union fund are halted. A specially formed council will
coordinate all actions of the 5,000 workforce. In the event of a worsening
political situation in the republic, fishermen will be joined by railway
workers from Primorye.

16.02. BANNED MEDIA CONTINUE TO WORK

MOSCOW (RIA). Last night, the Russian Supreme Soviet radio
service began broadcasting. It is being broadcast from the parliament
building on 1,500 khz medium wave.

Today, at 13.40, the Echo of Moscow radio station resumed broadcasting on 1,206 khz. According to RIA, Echo of Moscow also plans to
begin broadcasting on short wave.

The editorial board of Moscow News is preparing a 16 page issue. It
would probably be a joint publication with journalists from newspapers
banned by the new regime.

On Aug. 20, xerox copies of the newspapers Kuranty, Moscow News
and Megapolis Express appeared, as well as Komsomolskaya Pravda, which
has started operating as an information agency.

16.04. IS GORBACHEV IN MOSCOW?

MOSCOW (RIA). According to unconfirmed reports, Mikhail
Gorbachev arrived in Moscow in the second half of the day and is in his seat
in the Kremlin. He will probably make a statement on TV on the next day.

Meanwhile, at the USSR President's press service, where an RIA correspondent asked for a clarification, none of the officials, except for the secretary of the president's adviser, was available. Arkadi Maslennikov, head of the USSR Supreme Soviet press centre, announced that this information did not correspond to reality and that he knew nothing about the supposed Gorbachev speech on television. Meanwhile, the concentration of troops in the capital continues.

**16.11. ASSAULT OF THE WHITE HOUSE POSSIBLE THIS EVENING**
MOSCOW (RIA). According to RIA from confidential sources, troops obeying the State Emergency Committee will attempt an assault upon the Russian parliament building this evening. According to information from the same sources, one of the military units preparing for this operation is situated at the moment not far from the centre of Moscow and is armed with sniper rifles with night-sights.

**16.24. NAVAL TELECOMMUNICATIONS WORKERS READY TO PROVIDE CONNECTION TO THE WHITE HOUSE**
MOSCOW (RIA). "We are able to help Boris Yeltsin by ensuring long-distance radio and telecommunications broadcasts from the White House," said to an RIA correspondent Anatoli Grudnin, a captain of the second rank reserve. In his words, effectives of the central communications radio station of naval aviation of the USSR Military Naval Fleet are ready to provide connection via the USSR VMF satellite. This offer is being examined by Col. Gen. Kobets, Chairman of Russia's State Committee for Defence.

**16.28. GAVRIL POPOV'S SPEECH AT RALLY**
MOSCOW (RIA). On Aug. 20, Mayor of Moscow Gavril Popov addressed Muscovites at a rally. "Any organs that try to govern the city apart from those legally elected by Muscovites will be declared self-proclaimed and illegal," he said. "Anyone who creates such organs or agrees to work in them will bear criminal responsibility," Gavril Popov mentioned the criminal responsibility of head officials for carrying out orders of anticonstitutional organs, referring to the State Emergency Committee. He also warned managers of Moscow enterprises and organizations of the Union subordination of the criminal responsibility for carrying out orders given by the State Emergency Committee. The Mayor of Moscow stressed that any social organizations using Moscow territory and Moscow premises which support the anticonstitutional putsch would lose their right to operate on the territory of Moscow.
MOSCOW (PF). The All-Union Association of Development and Improvement of Ethnic Relations welcomes the State Emergency Committee statement and supports its realistic ideas expressing the will of Soviet

people, deeply angered by the demagogy under the guise of democracy, concealing lawlessness and condemning people to complete defenceless-ness.

David Feldstein,
President of the Association,
Professor of the Institute of Psychology, Academy of Pedagogical
Sciences

16.35. RUSSIAN COMMERCIAL ENTERPRISES ANNOUNCE AN INDEFINITE STRIKE
MOSCOW (RIA). A mass rally that began today at 12.00 at the Russian parliament building lasted more than three hours. It was announced at the rally that all Russian commercial enterprises would declare a general indefinite strike as of Aug. 20.

16.39. "DICTATORSHIP WILL NOT SUCCEED," HOPES EDUARD SHEVARDNADZE
MOSCOW (RIA). "The State Emergency Committee expresses the will of reactionaries of every shape and colour," said Eduard Shevardnadze in a speech at the rally at the White House on Aug. 20. In his opinion, the coup signifies the beginning of civil war, bloody confrontations between nations and peoples, the end of peaceful coexistence and a new spiralling of the arms race. But the former Soviet Foreign Minister believes the dictator-ship will not succeed.

16.51. ASSAULT ON THE PARLIAMENT BUILDING EXPECTED SOON
MOSCOW (RIA). The radio service of the Russian parliament has just informed of Sergei Stankevich's statement that there may soon be an assault on the parliament building on the Krasnopresnenskaya Embank-ment. In this connection, women in the building have been offered to leave the building in the fifteen minutes.
TAGANROG (PF). On Aug. 20, the presidium of the Taganrog City Soviet passed a resolution considering the forcible removal of USSR President Gorbachev from power and the formation of the State Emergency Committee as an anticonstitutional coup and its decrees as invalid.
KAMENSK-URALSK (PF). At an emergency meeting of the city Soviet Presidium, the removal of Gorbachev from power, the formation of the State Emergency Committee and the introduction of a state of emer-gency were declared illegal and anticonstitutional actions. The presidium considers it necessary to comply with the decrees of Russian President Boris Yeltsin and to obey the laws of the Russian Federation.
KHANTY-MANSIISK (PF). In an interview to PF, Mikhail Gromov, chairman of Khanty-Mansiisk City Soviet, said that the change in the

country's leadership was another attempt at revenge undertaken by a military-political grouping.

### 16.55. BORIS YELTSIN'S MEETING WITH EDUARD SHEVARDNADZE

MOSCOW (RIA). A meeting took place today at the White House on Krasnopresnenskaya Embankment between Russian President Boris Yeltsin and former Soviet Foreign Minister Eduard Shevardnadze who was accompanied by a group of close advisers. They talked about coordinating efforts for the restoration of law and order in the country.

### 17.00. TROOPS OF THE FAR EAST MILITARY DISTRICT REMAIN IN THEIR BARRACKS

KHABAROVSK (RIA). An official representative of the Far East military command announced that troops remained in their place of billeting. They were engaged in military training and guard duty.

Meanwhile, according to an RIA correspondent, from sources close to the district command, officers on leave received an order to return to their place of service.

### 17.06. YELTSIN'S TELEPHONE CONVERSATION WITH BUSH

MOSCOW (RIA). The Russain President's secretary, Pavel Voshchanov, announced that today, at 15.15 Moscow time, US President George Bush telephoned Boris Yeltsin. The US President asked about the situation in the USSR and the Russian Federation and the steps that the Russian leadership was taking to restore law and order.

Boris Yeltsin informed George Bush about the events, the decisions that had been taken and appeals by the Russian leadership, as well as plans for future action. Bush informed Yeltsin of talks between the "G7" leaders and heads of former socialist states. All those who had spoken with Bush unconditionally support Gorbachev and Yeltsin and thank the Russian President for his courage.

The USA and the world community intend in the near future to work out a series of measures for facilitating the restoration of rule of law in the USSR.

George Bush announced that the US leadership was not considering official recognition of the Yanayev administration.

### 17.13. TENSION IN MOSCOW INCREASES, ASSAULT ON MOSCOW CITY SOVIET POSSIBLE

MOSCOW (RIA). According to information received by an RIA correspondent at the Commission for Emergency Situations under the Moscow City Soviet, there has been a sharp increase in tension in Moscow since 16.00. Active troop movements have been observed around the city.

Furthermore, the Moscow City Soviet has received information that an assault on its headquarters had been set for 20.00. The Mayor of Moscow and the Moscow City Soviet intend to appeal to Muscovites to come to the Moscow City Soviet building by that time in order, without taking part in the conflict, to witness the possible bloodshed.

### 17.19. THE STATE EMERGENCY COMMITTEE DECLARED ILLEGAL BY DECREE OF THE MOLDOVAN PRESIDENT

KISHINEV (RIA). By decree of the Moldovan President, Mirchi Snegur, the State Emergency Committee, having carried out a state coup, is declared illegal. All decisions passed by the State Emergency Committee are considered illegal and invalid on the territory of Moldova. The decree stresses that only the legally elected bodies--parliament, president and government of Moldova--are effective in Moldova. The decree states the necessity of appealing to the leaders of the Union republics to pool efforts for the defence and support of constitutional order in the country and of condemning the actions of the State Emergency Committee, informs Moldova Press.

TYUMEN (PF). The majority of local government bodies on the territory of the Tyumen Region stated that they would obey the orders of the Russian leadership.

UFA (PF). In an Aug. 20 appeal to the population of Bashkiria, Murtaz Rakhimov, Chairman of the Bashkirian SSR Supreme Soviet, called for calm and normal work. Rakhimov said that a state of emergency would not be introduced in Bashkiria, therefore there was no reason for anxiety or panic. He said the situation was being controlled by the corresponding organs.

ROSTOV-ON-DON (PF). A meeting of the presidium of the Rostov-on-Don City Soviet was held on 20 August, at which it was decided to obey to the legally elected Russian government. In the centre of the city, next to the Rostov-on-Don City Soviet, a meeting of protest against the introduction of a state of emergency was organized by the Democratic Russia. About 600 people took part in the meeting. At the headquarters of the Northern-Caucausus military district it was announced that troops would carry out the orders of the State Emergency Committee.

### 17.25. THE MAJORITY OF MUSCOVITES DO NOT SUPPORT INTRODUCTION OF A STATE OF EMERGENCY

MOSCOW (RIA). On Aug. 20, an opinion poll was conducted from 1,500 Muscovites. Ten per cent of those polled expressed full or partial support for the State Emergency Committee and the introduction of a state of emergency, 79.4 per cent expressed their opposition. Only 3.9 per cent of those polled trusted Gennadi Yanayev as USSR acting president, 2.3 per cent for Valentin Pavlov as Prime Minister, whilst 53 per cent of those polled stated that Mikhail Gorbachev should return to his duties as USSR President. A very high level of support (82 per cent) was registered for Russian President Boris Yeltsin.

Although 72 per cent expressed their support for the restoration of order in the country, 64 per cent consider that this should be done by constitutional organs of power. 59 per cent suggested that the activities of the State Emergency Committee would merely lead to increaseing disorder and chaos in the country.

## 17.28. DEFENCE OF THE RUSSIAN PARLIAMENT BUILDING WILL BE STRENGTHENED

MOSCOW (RIA). According to information from the State Committee for Defence of the Russian Federation, 6 battalions of units stationed in the Leningrad Region (about 2,500 men, with weapons) are ready for movement to Moscow for the defence of the Russian parliament. Units made up of volunteers and Afghan war veterans will join them. Their transfer to Moscow will be carried out as soon as they receive air transportation.

## 17.44. BORIS YELTSIN'S SPEECH AT THE RALLY AT THE WHITE HOUSE

MOSCOW (RIA). "The junta, which has come to power, will stop at nothing to maintain this power," said Russian President Boris Yeltsin at the rally on Aug. 20 at the White House. "The members of the junta understand that if the worst comes to the worst they not only will lose their posts but will also sit on the bench of the accused."

Yeltsin called upon Russians not to carry out the decisions of the State Emergency Committee and announced that the procurator's office and the Interior Ministry of the republic had been given the order to bring criminal charges against anyone who obeyed the orders of this committee. He thanked Muscovites for their support and drew the attention of those gathered to the fact that a state of emergency was only introduced in those places where the supporters of democracy hold power. The Russian President called upon participants in the rally to remain calm and cautioned them against provocation of troops--"the blind tools are in the hands of the putchists". " I am convinced," said Boris Yeltsin "that aggression in democratic Moscow will fail."

## 17.48. THE RUSSIAN PRESIDENT HAS TAKEN COMMAND OVER THE WHOLE TERRITORY OF THE RSFSR

MOSCOW (RIA). Russian President Boris Yeltsin has assumed the duty of Chief-in-Command of the Armed Forces on the whole territory of the Russian Federation. In a decree signed by him today, it is stated that he will perform functions connected with this post until the USSR President, Mikhail Gorbachev, returns to his duties.

17.55. YELTSIN'S TELEPHONE CONVERSATION WITH MAJOR MOSCOW (RIA). President of the Russian Federation Boris Yeltsin was telephoned by British Prime Minister John Major on Aug. 20 at 17.00 Moscow time. Yeltsin informed Major of the situation in Russia in connection with the coup and about the measures taken by the Russian leadership. Yeltsin told Major about the planned assault on the Russian parliament building, which, in his words, was worked out by the KGB and the USSR Ministry of Defence. He received an assurance that, if this occurred in Russia, the world community would take decisive steps against the putchists. Today, as with the United States, Britain is also not considering the issue of official recognition of the Yanyaev administration.

KHABAROVSK (PF). It has become known that a few hours before the announcement of a state of emergency the headquarters of the Far East military district received a telegram from the Chief Political Administration of the Soviet Armed Forces warning them about this. Earlier, Victor Novozhilov, the Commander of the Far East military district said, that he did not know anything about the change in Union leadership. On the night of Aug. 20 a telegram was sent to the Far East border district from the Military Council of the USSR KGB border troops stating that "border troops must support the measures of the State Emergency Committee, defend the Soviet power and maintain the inviolability of its borders". All border checkpoints in the Far East border district were closed. On Aug. 20, another telegram was received from Moscow and signed by the Head of the USSR KGB border troops, Col. Gen. Ilya Kalinichenko, the Head of the Political Administration of the USSR KGB Border Troops, Lt. Gen. Nikolai Britvin and the secretary of the Russian Communist Party Committee of the USSR KGB border troops, Col. Vladimir Antsupov. The telegram was passed on to all heads of posts in the Far East border district with the demand that "every soldier and officer be acquainted with the resolutions of the State Emergency Committee and that they be convinced of the correctness of these decisions". Chairman of the Khabarovsk Territory Executive Committee Valeri Litvinov recommended that journalists only issue information provided by the State Emergency Committee.

According to observers, representatives of the Khabarovsk Territory exchanges divided into two camps. The general director of the Khabarovsk Commodity and Stock Exchange, Bizon, Yevgeni Shulepov said: "The response to the events is disgusting." The executive director of the Khabarovsk Commodity Exchange, Yevgeni Panasenko said: "I don't give a damn about Yeltsin and the others, I don't have the time, I'm involved in earning capital. And I don't intend to get involved in politics." On Aug. 20, a meeting of trade union leaders of the Khabarovsk Teeritory was held at which the decision was taken to call out onto the streets the workers of all enterprises on Aug. 21 at 20.00 and to compel the presidium of the territory Soviet to support Yeltsin. The Khabarovsk Department of the Central Bank of Russia suspended all crediting operations for commercial structures. The stated reason was the absence of credit resources.

MAGADAN (PF). On the morning of Aug. 20, at a joint meeting of the regional Soviet and executive committee, the decision was taken to support Yeltsin and to implement his decrees. Yeltsin's opinion that a coup has taken place in the country was supported. The acting procurator of the Magadan Region, Prokhorov, was the only one to condemn Yeltsin's actions. Regional Interior chief Vladimir Povazhny said that the local police would obey the orders of the Russian Interior Ministry.

18.12. PRESIDENT OF KAZAKHSTAN'S SPEECH ON REPUBLICAN TELEVISION
ALMA-ATA (RIA). The President of Kazakhstan, Nursultan Nazarbayev, called for an immediate session of the USSR Supreme Soviet which must consider the issue of calling an extraordinary Congress of People's Deputies of the USSR within the next ten days. Speaking on republican TV, he called to determine a definite date for all-Union election of the USSR President at the Supreme Soviet session. "The situation in the country demanded immediate intervention," he said. "However, the introduction of a state of emergency could only be declared on a constitutional, legal basis." President Nazarbayev believes the USSR President, Mikhail Gorbachev, must personally confirm his inability to carry out his duties.

MOSCOW (PF). Speaking on internal radio in the Russian parliament building, the President of Russia's adviser, Sergei Stankevich said: "I would like to inform you about the events that took place on August 19t at the presidential dacha at Foros in the Crimea. On August 19, from 4 a.m. the runway at Belbek, where President Gorbachev's TU-134 airplane and MI-8 Helicopter were situated, was blocked by two trucks. This was done on the orders of Gen. Maltsev, Chief of Staff of the country's air defence forces. All actions for blocking the presidential dacha were carried out by Sevastopol regiment of KGB troops, which now has complete control over the dacha. At 10.42, attempts were made to move the TU-134 and MI-8 from the airfield. Then an order was given by Gen. Yesimsky to take a group of nine servicemen aboard an aircraft. The group,however, did not appeart. At 18.43, on the order of the head of the operations administration of the headquarters, Gen. Denisov, the following people were permitted to be taken on board the aircraft: Kozlov, Gubernatorov, Alexandrova and Sorokina. Gubernatorov is known as one of the president's personal body guards, Alexandrova and Sorokina are his personal stenographic secretaries, who work directly with the president. The KGB checked all their documents and they were taken on board. At 19.38, the aircraft took off for Vnukovo airport. The captain of the TU-134 crew was Kalugin. The president's means of communication were taken out on this flight. I appeal to any Muscovites who know Gubernatorov, Alexandrova, Sokorina or Kozlov, anyone who can say anything about their whereabouts. Please telephone the Russian parliament and inform the Russian government. At 21.00, the MI-8 helicopter was forced to fly to Simferopol. THe captain of the crew was Vassiliev. Earlier, an attempt was made to fly it to Zaporozhye but according to our information, they were refused permission there. The runway remained blocked. Information has come from troops, that the political department has created operative groups for guarding, during the period of operations connected with the implementation of the state of emergency. All information that is given to these groups is passed on to Col. Gen. Boiko, also a member of the PVO command. We are possessing information and I cannot divulge where the group of aircraft flew off from, where they landed and where they set off for. The sky in the south is completely blocked, as is the case with the sea. Up to sixteen vessels have been sent to the east from the Cape of Foros. From 16.00, Aug. 19, all flights, sailing and travel to the dacha at Cape Foros has been prohibited. At 14.30, there was information from Moscow that the large aircraft ordered for the president will not take off for Gorbachev. President Gorbachev had ordered it two days before, intending to fly to Moscow on Aug. 19. At 15.10, Aug. 19, the following verbal order was given by Col. Gen. Maltsev: "Attempts have been made by those close to the former president to force their way through to Gorbachev. I give the order that in the event of repeated attempts, all individuals be detained and handed over to the KGB." Together with President Gorbachev at the dacha at Foros are Gen. Medvedev, head of the president's personal body guards, Chernyayev and Shakhnazarovh, presedential advisers. Together with Shakhnazarov there are his wife, Anna Shakhnazarova and their son, Karen Shakhnazarov, the well-known film director. They were staying with Shakhnazarov at the Yuzhny sanatorium not far from Foros," said Sergei Stankevich. At 17.30, at a meeting of the presidium of the Russian Supreme Soviet contacts between members of the Russian leadership and Anatoli Lukyanov were discussed. It was stressed that there was a real threat of an assault on the Russian parliament building.

18.25. YANAEV SAYS HE KNOWS NOTHING ABOUT A POSSIBLE ASSAULT ON THE RUSSIAN PARLIAMENT
     MOSCOW (RIA). After the Russiann President received information about a planned assault on the White House on Krasnopresnenskaya Embankment, his closest colleagues, on his orders, made contact with

Chairman of the USSR Supreme Soviet Anatoli Lukyanov, who informed them that he had spoken to Dmitri Yazov and Vladimir Kryuchkov and both of them had denied any knowledge of such plans.

Afterwards, according to information from the President's press service, Gennadi Yanayev telephoned the Russian president. Boris asked him: "So you want to take the White House? Do you realize the consequences for you in this country and abroad?" To which came the following reply: "I don't know anything about it. I'll look into it and if this is the case, then I will cancel the order."

## 18.33. THE STATE EMERGENCY COMMITTEE IS NOT SUPPORTED IN SEVERODVINSK

SEVERODVINSK (RIA). The printing of newspapers and broadcast of radio programmes has been resumed in the town without prior arrangement. The mass media are making public all information coming from the Russian government. The situation in the town is under the complete control of the mayor.

## 18.50. AN EMERGENCY SESSION OF THE MOSCOW CITY SOVIET TO BE CALLED ON AUGUST 22

MOSCOW (RIA). The presidium of Moscow City Soviet decided to call its emergency session on Aug. 22. The district Soviets of Moscow and their executive committees are instructed "to ensure the strict compliance with Russian President Yeltsin's decrees No. 59 and 61 of Aug. 19," and "to take all necessary steps for the guaranteeing of the continued functioning of essential services in the city".

## 18.54. TROOPS ARE STATIONED NEAR GATCHINA

LENINGRAD (RIA). According to information from the regional Interior department, as before a regiment of armoured infantry of the Pskov airborne division, which arrived there at 10 a.m. is still stationed near Gatchina, about 60 kilometres from Leningrad. In general, these soldiers are in their first year of service. They have no connection with the outside world, apart from internal army portable transmitter sets. The core of the Pskov division is moving towards Tallinn.

## 19.03. THE USSR UNION OF JOURNALISTS PROTESTS AGAINST THE INFRINGEMENT OF GLASNOST

MOSCOW (RIA). The USSR Union of Journalists expressed vigorous protest against the banning of a range of editions, TV and radio programmes in its statement of Aug. 20. The leaders of the union, including the committee for the defence of freedom of speech and journalists' rights, consider that this ban violates existing laws and leasd to a worsening situation in the future. Demanding the lifting of the ban, the Union of Journalists called upon Soviet and foreign journalists to display solidarity with their colleagues, whose rights and possibly even personal safety are under threat. The union called upon journalists to carry out their professional duty and expects that the USSR Supreme Soviet will cancel the anticonstitutional decisions, that have encroached upon the rights and freedoms of citizens.

**19.12. RUSSIAN COSSACKS ARMING THEMSELVES TO DEFEND YELTSIN AND GORBACHEV**

MOSCOW (RIA). The head of the State Committee for Defence of the Russian Federation, Konstantin Kobets, sent the commander-in-chief of Cossack forces in Russia, Mikhail Nesmachny, to the horse regiment of Mosfilm studios in the village of Golitsyno to receive horses and weapons essential to Cossacks for the defence of Russian President Boris Yeltsin and the legitimate government of the USSR headed by the USSR President, Mikhail Gorbachev.

MOSCOW (PF). According to information of the Russian leadership at 19.00, forty tanks are moving from Kalinisky Prospekt. A KGB regiment has been stationed outside the Rossiya Hotel, out of other forces that are on the move there is information about an armored tank division and the movement of airborne regiments. Live broadcasts of Echo of Moscow and Radio Rossiya are being transmitted from the Russian parliament building.

**19.20. RUSSIAN PRESIDENT'S DECREE ON THE APPOINTMENT OF A COMMANDER OF THE LENINGRAD MILITARY DISTRICT**

MOSCOW (RIA). On Aug. 20, Russian President Boris Yeltsin signed a Decree on the appointment of commander of the Leningrad military district. The document states:

"For the organization and administration of all military units and formations on the territory of the Leningrad military district, I decree that:

"1. Until the complete restoration of the activities of constitutional organs and institutions of state power and administration, Rear-Admiral Vyacheslav Shcherbakov shall be appointed commander of Leningrad military district.

"2. All military units and formations of the USSR Armed Forces, troops of the USSR KGB and the USSR Interior Ministry stationed on the territory of the Leningrad military district, shall carry out the orders and instructions of the commander of the Leningrad military district, Rear-Admiral Shcherbakov.

"3. The State Committee for Defence of the Russian Federation shall be informed of all decisions to be taken on the territory of Leningrad military district.

"4. This Decree shall come into effect as of the moment of its signing. RSFSR President B. Yeltsin"

### 19.35. RUSSIAN PRESIDENT'S DECREE ON APPOINTMENT OF RSFSR MINISTER OF DEFENCE

MOSCOW (RIA). On Aug. 20 August Russian President Boris Yeltsin signed a decree on the appointment of the RSFSR Minister of Defence:

"To ensure accurate coordination of the administration of troops and the prevention of the use of troops against civilians, I decree that: "Until the complete restoration of the activities of constitutional organs and institutions of state power and administration, the Chairman of the RSFSR State Defence Committee, General Konstantin Kobets shall be appointed the RSFSR Minister of Defence.

*RSFSR President Boris Yeltsin"*

### 19.45. PROTEST MEETING HELD IN VLADIVOSTOK

VLADIVOSTOK (RIA). "We will restore legal power!", "No to the military-party coup!"--the inhabitants of Vladivostok came out to the protest meeting with such banners on Aug. 20. Those who spoke called for civil disobedience in response to the decisions of the State Emergency Committee, for a general strike in the city and the restoration of power of the legitimate USSR President Mikhail Gorbachev. Participants in the meeting sent a telegram to Russian President Boris Yeltsin expressing support for his actions.

### 19.57. THE POLITICAL ADMINISTRATION OF THE VDV DENIES RUMOURS OF THE ARREST OF THE COMMANDER OF LANDING TROOPS

MOSCOW (RIA). An official of the Political Administration of the Airborne Troops, Gennadi Sinkov, denied rumours that the Commander of the Airborne Troops, Gen. Pavel Grachev, had been arrested allegedly in connection with the fact that a unit of landing troops had gone over to Boris Yeltsin's side. He also informed that sub-divisions of the VDV numbering up to three thousand men had been removed from their former places of stationing in Moscow and had been concentrated in Tushino. A company of landing troops was also situated in other places in Moscow, said the Lt. Colonel.

### 20.10. STATEMENT OF THE LITHUANIAN SUPREME SOVIET

VILNIUS (RIA). The Supreme Soviet of the Lithuanian Republic issued a statement, in which it vigorously condemned the attempt to overthrow the legally and democratically elected Russian government, introduce a military dictatorship and sink democracy in Russia and other republics of the Soviet Union in blood, informs the Elta agency. The statement stresses that the forces which are now acting are the same forces which tried to overthrow the democratically elected government of Lithuania on January 13, 1991.

"Then, the Russia's leadership, its deputies and citizens stood vigorously on the side of Lithuania. Today, we express our solidarity with all the progressive forces in Russia and vigorously support all your efforts to defend fundamental human rights and freedoms,'' states the document.

20.13. MEETING IN SUPPORT OF THE RUSSIAN AUTHORITIES IN LENINGRAD

LENINGRAD (RIA). From 10 a.m. to 1.00 p.m. a meeting of protest was held on Palace Square in Leningrad, which had been announced on television by Anatoli Sobchak the day before.

According to the Interior department estimates, there had never been so many people gathered on the square; more than 300,000 Leningraders expressed their attitude towards the putschists. A column of 10,000 people went out onto the square at Kirov works. A group of "Afghantsi" (Afghan war veterans) also went out onto the square, stating their loyalty to the Russian parliament. Amongst the speakers at the meeting were: Anatoli Sobchak, Alexander Belov, Marina Sale, academic Dmitri Likhachev and an official representative of the Orthodox Church, who blessed those gathering.

Almost every speech ended with the slogan "Fascism will not succeed!" The meeting unanimously accepted a declaration of support of the decrees of the Russian parliament, the decisions of Leningrad City Soviet and the Mayor of Leningrad.

When the meeting had finished, many of the participants went to the Leningrad City Soviet building in order to guarantee its protection.

20.37. PRESIDENT OF TATARSTAN SUPPORTS THE STATE EMERGENCY COMMITTEE

KAZAN (RIA). On 20 August in speech to the presidential council of the Tatar SSR, the President of the TSSR, Mintimer Shaimiev, supported the State Emergency Committee. He stated, that the orders of the Committee must be carried out on the territory of the republic. In an officially disseminated appeal of the President of Tatarstan to the people of the republic there was no mention of the State Emergency Committee, but it referred to the necessary of observing calm and working actively. The President of Tatarstan threatened violators of order with emergency measures. On 20 August, a protest meeting was held in Kazan against the anti-constitutional coup and in support of Yeltsin. Participants were broken up by detachments of the Interior task force.

In effect, censorship has been introduced into the republic--the director of the publishing house of the CPSU republican committee, Vladimir Gavrilov on Aug. 19 removed from the pages of an independent newspaper Vechernyaya Kazan the material which referred to the position of the leadership of Russia with regard to the State Emergency Committee.

**20.43. MOSCOW CITY SOVIET INFORMS: CURFEW WILL TAKE EFFECT IN MOSCOW FROM 23.00**
MOSCOW (RIA). "A curfew will be take effect in Moscow today from 23.00 and at the same time the withdrawal of troops from the capital will begin," said Nikolai Kalinin, the commander of Moscow Military District in a telephone conversation with Yuri Sharykin, member of the headquarters providing contacts of Moscow City Soviet with the Russian Parliament.

"I will announce this on the Vremya television programme or immediately afterwards," said Nikolai Kalinin.

**20.46. RUSSIAN FOREIGN MINISTRY STATEMENT**
MOSCOW (RIA). In a situation when state coup has been undertaken in the country, flouting both the constitutions of the USSR and RSFSR and human rights, the leadership of the Russia considers, that the holding of the third, final stage of the conference on human dimension within the frame-work of the common European process, set for Sept. 10 in Moscow is inexpedient. On Aug. 20, the Foreign Ministry of Russia appealed to the heads of all European states, the USA and Canada with a call to refuse to take part in the conference on human dimension of the CSCE. The statement stresses adherence of Russia to democratic ideals, a strict adherence to international legal standards and the observance of human rights.

**20.49. KUBAN COORDINATES ITS ACTIONS WITH THE STATE EMERGENCY COMMITTEE**
KRASNODAR (RIA). "The main task of the territorial Soviet is to maintain stability in the Kuban and to create the necessary conditions for calm and the well-being of citizens, to guarantee the working of all branches of the economy and in particular that of agricultural production. Political passions and the activities of public organizations must move to a secondary level," said Nikolai Kondratenko, chairman of the Territorial Soviet on Aug. 19 at a meeting with leaders of the media.

He talked about measures that had been taken in the territory in connection with the statement by the State Emergency Committee on the introduction of a state of emergency in individual districts of the USSR. Krasnodar Territorial Soviet of People's Deputies has set up a headquarters, which will interact with the State Emergency Committee as well as municipal district Soviets, in order to coordinate the actions of organs of state power.

ABAKAN (PF). The presidium of Abakan City Soviet supports the Russian leadership. This was decided at a meeting of the presidium of Abakan City Soviet on Aug 20. It was decided to declare the actions of the State Emergency Committee anticonstitutional and to observe the laws of Russia. The chairman of Abakan City Soviet, Alexander Karlov informed that the leaders of the CPSU city committee had offered him the opportunity of participating in the creation of a city emergency committee. It was also suggested that Karlov hand over all power to the secretary of the CPSU city committee.

The presidium of Khakass Soviet, at its meeting of Aug. 20 demanded, that Gorbachev be given the opportunity to speak before the population of the country. The Khakass authorities intend to be governed strictly by the existing laws of the RSFSR and USSR, rigorously carrying out the demands of the legally elected President of Russia, the Supreme Soviet and Council of Ministers of the Russian Federation.

The population in a range of cities in Siberia--Novosibirsk, Tomsk, Tyumen, Khanty-Mansiisk, Bratsk, Irkutsk, Abakan, Kyzyl, Barnaul, Krasnoyarsk and Norilsk are completely unaware of events taking place in Moscow. A multitude of rumours are being spread, that Gorbachev has been killed, that the Taman Division, a regiment of the Ryazan Division, Air Force and Air Defence Forces have moved over to Yeltsin's side. All this is taking place because of the absence of reliable sources of information. The population is listening to Western radio broadcasts, which continue to be jammed. It has become known, that the armed forces are jamming the broadcasts.


20.53. KARELIA WILL LIVE ACCORDING TO RUSSIAN LAWS

PETROZAVODSK (RIA). Karelian radio and television, which began working today, broadcast all decrees and appeals by the Russian President.
Then, the chairman of the Council of Ministers of Karelia, Sergei Blinnikov made a speech in which he informed that Karelia would live according to Russian laws.


20.56. PARTICIPANTS OF THE EXPATRIATES CONGRESS EXPRESS THEIR PROTEST

MOSCOW (RIA). Participants of the Congress of Expatriates applauded the announcement by the chairman of the organizational committee of the congress, People's Deputy of Russia, Mikhail Tolstoy, that several of the military units had moved onto the side of the Russian leadership.

*Citizens of Moscow have taken over a tank.*

*Funeral at the Vagan Kovski cemetery.*
*"Forgive me for not being able to protect your sons". B.N. Yeltsin*

*Soldiers of a tank division which has sided with the people.*

*There are no roars of of intense thunder. The infantrymen don't choke in rage, when people carry fresh flowers in their hands,*
*Tanks lose their purpose.*

*Moscow. The first assault on the "White House" has been repelled. Armoured personnel carriers of the army which hadn't been able to break through the blockade of trolley buses, turned away to the Kalinin prospect. Near the U.S. Embassy, two defenders of the Russian parliament were killed and a few others injured.*

*This bus blocked the progress of the tanks and was set on fire. Now the bus is part of the collection of the Museum of the Revolution.*

At a general meeting of the congress, participants decided to send a letter of protest to the USSR Supreme Soviet in connection with events in the country. At first, it was suggested that the letter be addressed to the State Emergency Committee. However, the majority rejected the possibility of any relations with this "illegal structure". A copy of the letter will be sent to the UN.

NOVOSIBIRSK (PF). Leaders of the largest factories of the military-industrial complex situated in Novosibirsk react very unfavourably towards the creation of the State Emergency Committee. The majority of business-men also react unfavourably to the removal of Gorbachev. The Asian Stock Exchange went on strike. The leaders of the Nizhnevartovsk Stock Exchange reacted very unfavourably to the State Emergency Committee. In several banks in Novosibirsk panic has been observed amongst clients.

## 21.04. PROGRAMME OF THE EXPATRIATES CONGRESS IN LENINGRAD WILL NOT BE CANCELLED

MOSCOW (RIA). The programme of the Congress of Expatriates in Leningrad will go ahead as planned. Participants of the congress were informed of this on Aug. 20. Their departure to Leningrad will take place on Aug. 20 in the evening. In connection with this, one of the foreign guests said: "We are pleased that we will be able to visit St. Petersburg after all. But we would like to know, whether or not we will be able to return afterwards?"

## 21.07. GREAT-GRANDSON OF LEO TOLSTOY ON EVENTS IN THE COUNTRY

MOSCOW (RIA). Relations between the USSR and the international community will become considerably more difficult in connection with the latest events. This was the opinion expressed to an RIA correspondent by Leo Tolstoy's great-grandson, Ilya Ivanovich Tolstoy, a businessman living in France, who took part in the Congress of Expatriates.

"We realized, that even though Gorbachev was a child of Marxism, he was a man with whom we could do business. Now, with his displacement, there is no trust in the Soviet Union anymore," said Ilya Tolstoy. In his opinion, members of the State Emergency Committee do not feel sufficiently secure in their position and it is precisely for this reason, that they hurried in their closing down of the media.

"Yesterday, during the press conference on television it was noticeable that the person sitting in the middle of the presidium was not confident, his hands were shaking," noticed the great-grandson of the great writer.

21.30. KAMCHATKA: THE AUTHORITIES CALL FOR A REJECTION
OF MASS DEMONSTRATIONS

PETROPAVLOVSK-KAMCHATSKY (RIA). The presidium of the
executive committee of Kamchatka Regional Soviet took the decision to
create a regional group on the state of emergency, which would study and
analyze the situation in the country. On Aug. 20, in an address to the
inhabitants of Kamchatka, the solidarity of the regional leadership with the
evaluation of events expressed by the Russian government and the USSR
Constitutional Supervisory Committee was stressed. The Soviet called
upon the population to refrain from strikes and other mass demonstrations.
On the same day, a joint address of the presidium and executive committee
of the regional Soviet and the military command of Kamchatka garrison was
agreed upon: ''We consider it necessary to state, that in the present situation
the firing up of passions and the incitement of the media is impermissible.''
The armed forces will cooperate with the local authorities for the maintenance of order in the region.

At the same time the independent television company TVK came on
the air in Kamchatka, broadcasting documents of the Russian leadership and
RIA information.

21.33. MAYOR AND VICE-MAYOR OF LENINGRAD'S TELEVISED
SPEECHES ON LOCAL TELEVISION

LENINGRAD (RIA). The Mayor of Leningrad, Anatoli Sobchak and
the Vice-Mayor, Vyacheslav Shcherbakov spoke on Aug. 20 on Leningrad
television. The Russian Presidential Decree on the appointment of Vyacheslav
Shcherbakov as representative of the RSFSR State Defence Committee was
read out. The headquarters of civil opposition, to be headed by the captain
of the first flotilla of nuclear submarines of the Northern Fleet, vice-admiral
Yevgeni Chernov was set up.

Vyacheslav Shcherbakov appealed to military personnel of the Leningrad military district with a call to make a choice in favour of the people
and to carry out the decrees of the Russian President. An oath demands
service to the people and not to a group of conspirators, said Vyacheslav
Shcherbakov. An emergency session of the city and regional Soviets is
continuing. Deputies are discussing the possibility of round the clock
television.

21.38. RSFSR PRESIDENT BORIS YELTSIN'S STATEMENT

MOSCOW (RIA). Boris Yeltsin made a statement which says: ''With
the aim of preventing an escalation of confrontation between society and the
army and the transformation into civil war, the exclusion of illegal, violent
actions against anyone I decree:

"Those individuals of the military and officials of the USSR Ministry of Defence, Ministry of the Interior and KGB involved in the anticonstitutional actions of the State Emergency Committee will not be brought to justice for the carrying out of decisions of their leaders, in the event of their swift and rigorous carrying out of decrees and orders of the RSFSR President, resolutions of the RSFSR Council of Ministers and other organs and officials of the RSFSR."

21.43. APPEAL OF THE GOVERNMENT OF RUSSIA TO LAW EN-FORCING ORGANS AND THE PEOPLE'S MILITIA
MOSCOW (RIA). The RSFSR government published the following appeal on Aug. 20:
Comrade officials of law enforcing organs, people's militia! In this difficult time for our mother country the legally elected leadership of Russia appeals to you with the call to maintain loyalty to the Russian people's legitimate government and loyalty to your people. We call upon to reject any participation whatsoever in the actions of the putschists. Maintain your courage and loyalty to your people. The fate of your mother country and the lives of your fellow countrymen depend to a great degree upon you!

21.44. THERE ARE NO TANKS IN THE KANTEMIR TANK DIVISION
MOSCOW (RIA). "We did not find any tanks when we visited the Kantemir tank division in the Naro-Fominsk District." This is what Moscow Regional Soviet Deputies Eduard Puzyrev and Alexander Kulakov, as well as Moscow City Soviet Deputy Sergei Shornikov had to say.
In the words of the deputies, the decrees and resolutions of Boris Yeltsin, which had been published over the last two days proved to be "news to us and interesting reading" for the service personnel in the unit. Naming no names, military personnel gave the information, that the tanks had left for Moscow.

21.47. MINISTRY OF DEFENCE DENIES INFORMATION ABOUT YAZOV'S RESIGNATION
MOSCOW (RIA). According to RIA, the USSR Defence Minister, Dmitri Yazov, has resigned. In this way he allegedly expressed his disagree-ment with the participation of the army in the removal of the legally elected authorities. He has been replaced in this post by Mikhail Moiseyev. Meanwhile, the head of the press service of the USSR Ministry of Defence, Valeri Manilov, who was approached by RIA for a clarification, stated that this information did not correspond to reality.

21.50. SAMARA SUPPORTS NEITHER THE STATE EMERGENCY COMMITTEE NOR THE RUSSIAN PRESIDENT

SAMARA (RIA). According to the information from the chairman of Samara Soviet of People's Deputies, V.A. Tarkhov, until an emergency session of the USSR Supreme Soviet is held, Samara Region and Samara intends neither to subordinate to the State Emergency Committee nor to support the Russian President, Boris Yeltsin. In agreement with General Makashov, not one military formation will have the right to take any actions on the territory of Samara and Samara Region without the direct instructions of the local authorities.

21.59. LENINGRAD OFFICERS DEMAND THE IMPLEMENTATION OF YELTSIN'S DECREES

LENINGRAD (RIA). Leningrad Military District is satisfied with the appointment of Vyacheslav Shcherbakov as commander of Leningrad Military District, as he is a competent man who has the trust of soldiers, Maj. Gen. Venedict Fyodorov, deputy chief of staff of Air Defence Forces of Leningrad Military District, told an RIA correspondent.

An appeal from the officers of the artillery courses was spread around Leningrad. The officers demand, that Mikhail Gorbachev be restored to the post of USSR President and that he be given the opportunity to speak publicly, that all troops in the Soviet Army are subordinate to him and that in the future they swear an oath of allegiance to USSR President, as well as implement the decree of the Russian President on prosecution of the conspirators according to law.

22.09. INDEPENDENT RUSSIAN TRADE UNIONS ON THE SITUA- TION IN THE COUNTRY

MOSCOW (RIA). In an address to the miners of Russia, the Inde- pendent Miners Union of Russia notes that the measures for stabilizing economic ties should only be acted upon with the strictest observance of the Constitution and the laws of the Russian Federation, without any attempt to flout the rights and authority of the President and Supreme Soviet of Russia.

The presidium of the Council of Moscow Federation of Unions demanded the withdrawal of troops from Moscow, the swiftest calling of a session of the Supreme Soviet of the USSR and the resolution of the situation through constitutional means.

Tyumen Regional Council of Unions called on the workers not to get involved in political games; however, it did express a negative attitude in relation to the introduction of a state of emergency.

TOBOLSK (PF). On Aug. 20, the presidium of Tobolsk City Soviet came out in support of the decision by Tyumen Regional Soviet on unconditional implementation of the decrees of the Russian President, declaring the creation of the State Emergency Committee illegal. Representatives of the KGB and the Department of the Interior stressed their readiness to carry out the orders of the regional leadership.

## 22.12. ADDRESS OF THE PRESIDENT OF UNITED COOPERATORS TO COOPERATORS AND BUSINESSMEN OF THE SOVIET UNION

MOSCOW (RIA). The President of United Cooperators, Academician Vladimir Tikhonov addressed cooperators and businessmen of the Soviet Union. In his address it is stated that what is taking place is an attempted coup d'etat, carried out by a group of irresponsible adventurists. These people are doomed, claims Vladimir Tikhonov, but they are hoping for the support of reactionary forces, therefore, it is essential to begin with a decisive and uncompromising struggle for the preservation of all achievements in the field of free enterprise. On behalf of the leadership of United Cooperators, Tikhonov called upon cooperators and businessmen to begin active opposition to the putschists' actions.

"We call upon you to boycott the actions of the officials carrying out the decisions of the State Emergency Committee," writes Academician Tikhonov. "We call upon you to actively support strikes and other forms of political struggle."

## 22.15. KALININGRAD CITY SOVIET EXPRESSES ADHERENCE TO THE RUSSIAN LEADERS

KALININGRAD (RIA). The presidium of Kaliningrad City Soviet of People's Deputies made an appeal to the population, in which it condemned the unconstitutional methods of the displacement of USSR President Mikhail Gorbachev from his post, expressed adherence to the Constitution and the Russian President and called upon inhabitants to remain calm.

The legally elected Soviet authorities continue to act in the city. Activists of the local organization of the Russian Democratic Party are distributing leaflets with an appeal of the Russian leadership to the people and are gathering signatures in support of the Russian President.

## 22.37. ORDER OF THE RUSSIAN DEFENCE MINISTER NO. 1

MOSCOW (RIA). Order of the RSFSR Minister of Defence No. 1. Aug. 20, 1991, Moscow:

In execution of the RSFSR Presidential Decrees of Aug. 19, 1991, No. 61, and of Aug. 20, 1991, No. 67, I ORDER:

Commanders of district troops, fleets, armies and flotillas, commanding officers of formations and units, heads of etablishments, military institutions, enterprises and organizations of the USSR Ministry of Defence, located on the territory of the Russian Federation, territorial, regional, city and district military commissariats on the territory of the Russian Federation:

do not permit the implementation of any decisions and orders of the anticonstitutional State Emergency Committee;

exclude all possibilities of using troops and fleet forces against the civilian population and legally elected organs of state authority; take swift measures to ensure the return of subordinate troops and fleet forces to areas of permanent dislocation and ensure the continuation of their training.

Implementation should be communicated through commanders of military districts by 06.00, Aug. 21, 1991.

*RSFSR Minister of Defence Colonel General K. Kobets*

**22.43. ORDER OF THE RUSSIAN DEFENCE MINISTER NO. 2 "ON THE CANCELLATION OF CURFEW IN MOSCOW"**

MOSCOW (RIA). Order of the RSFSR Minister of Defence No. 2. Aug. 20, 1991, Moscow:

In connection with information about the proposed assault on the White House of Russia by officers of the USSR KGB during the operation of curfew in Moscow, in accordance with the powers invested in me by the RSFSR Presidential Decree, I ORDER:

1. To cancel the decision to introduce a curfew in Moscow.

2. All sub-units, services and citizens taking part in the defence of the Russian parliament, to maintain endurance and a high level of vigilance.

*RSFSR Minister of Defence Colonel General K. Kobets*

**22.48. LVOV READY TO SUPPORT THE RUSSIAN PRESIDENT**

MOSCOW (RIA). "All enterprises in Lvov Region are ready to go on strike in response to the call of the Russian President,' said Gennadi Stasyuk, one of the leaders of the Lvov organization of Rukh.

In a telephone interview with an RIA correspondent in Moscow, he informed, that on Aug. 19, the regional organization of Rukh made an appeal to the inhabitants of Lvov Region, in which the current events were characterized as an anticonstitutional coup with the aim of suppressing the democratic movement for perestroika. The appeal contains a call for unification of all democratic forces and a boycott of decrees from the anticonstitutional organs that have come to power as a result of the coup.

**22.51. CALLS FOR CIVIL DISOBEDIENCE**

MOSCOW (RIA). The most varied of political parties, organizations and movements are calling for the unification of all antitotalitarian forces. In particular, on Aug. 20 an appeal of the Republican Party of the Russian Federation and the coordinating council of the Moscow organization of the Democratic Union--"Grazhdansky Put" Party was distributed. As a means of struggling against the State Emergency Committee they suggest organizing a campaign of civil disobedience, the calling of strikes and other nonviolent actions.

22.59. BORIS YELTSIN'S APPEAL TO THE TROOPS OF THE TAMAN MOTORIZED RIFLE DIVISION, DZERZHINSKY DETACHED MOTORIZED RIFLE DIVISION, KANTEMIR TANK DIVISION

MOSCOW (RIA). Fellow countrymen! Soldiers! Sons!

I, the Russian President, elected by the will of our suffering people, appeal to you at this difficult moment for our fatherland. There is a choice before you: either you give support to the group of conspirators, usurpers of power and carry their criminal order and thus go against the will of the people, or you defend democracy and power legally elected by the people.

The first path will lead the country into a fratricidal civil war and severe bloodshed. The second path guarantees civil peace and constitutional order and security.

My dear Sons! I am relying upon you, upon your correct choice. I hope that you will stand on the side of legal power, that of the President of Russia. I am convinced that you will not permit violence, that your mothers and fathers will not be embittered by their children.

Fellow countrymen! Soldiers of the Taman, Dzerzhinsky and Kantemir divisions!

I give you the order: quickly without hesitation come over to the side of legal power, observing with this order and discipline.

The humiliation and insult of great Russia is calling you.

*Boris Yeltsin*

23.02. ADDRESS OF THE PRESIDENT OF THE REPUBLIC OF GEORGIA TO THE PEOPLES AND GOVERNMENTS OF WESTERN COUNTRIES

MOSCOW (RIA). In the address of Aug. 20 the President of the Republic of Georgia, Zviad Gamsakhurdia, in connection with the "coup that has taken place" called upon Western governments, in particular, the USA, to urgently de facto and de jure recognize the independence of the republics of the USSR, "which are struggling for their independence and possess parliaments and presidents elected by the people". He also called for the establishing of diplomatic relations with them, which, in his opinion, should defend those peoples moving towards democracy. At the same time doubts are expressed in his address of the sincerity of the coup, the suspicion that it is merely "a fraud, or a show for the acquisition of political dividends, on which several leaders are counting on".

23.08. PARLIAMENTS OF ESTONIA AND LATVIA: THE EXIST-
ENCE OF THE STATE EMERGENCY COMMITTEE IS UNCONSTI-
TUTIONAL

MOSCOW (RIA). The Chairman of the Supreme Soviet of Estonia,
Arnold Ruutel met on Aug. 20 with the deputy commander of troops of the
Baltic Military District, Lt. Gen. Fyodor Melnichuk. An RIA correspondent
was informed of this by the press attache of the Chairman of the Supreme
Soviet of Estonia, Leivi Sher.

Threatening the introduction of a state of emergency in the republic,
the general demanded the implementation of resolution No. 1 of the State
Emergency Committee, in particular, the prohibition of meetings, strikes
and other actions, as well as the removal of barricades from Vyshgorod. In
reply, Arnold Ruutel said that the Estonian Supreme Soviet considered the
seizure of power by the State Emergency Committee unconstitutional and
that Estonia would continue the struggle for the restoration of independence
through political means and in any conditions.

A state of emergency has been introduced in Latvia. There are
casualties informs the Baltia agency. The Latvian parliament lays all
responsibility for the consequences of illegal actions with the commander
of the Baltic Military District, Col. Gen. Fyodor Kuzmin, representative of
the State Emergency Committee in the Baltics. The parliament of the
republic appealed to the USSR Supreme Soviet with the demand of the
immediate calling of the Congress of People's Deputies, the cancellation of
the resolution on the introduction of a state of emergency as unconstitutional, halting the activities of the State Emergency Committee on the
territory of Latvia and bringing the guilty parties to justice.

23.11. ORDER OF THE MAYOR OF MOSCOW

MOSCOW (RIA). On Aug. 20, the Mayor of Moscow gave the order
"On the activities of public organizations and the suspending of the
activities of Moscow organizations of war and labour veterans":

"The All-Union Council of War and Labour Veterans and the Soviet
Committee of Veterans of the War in the name of these public organizations
distributed a statement of support for the self-proclaimed State Emergency
Committee, which has been organized by a group of state criminals.

'In accordance with the decree issued by RSFSR President Boris
Yeltsin on the unconstitutional State Emergency Committee and the
criminal responsibility of its members and those that carry out its orders:

'1. The government of Moscow (Yu. M. Luzhkov) is taking steps to
temporarily halt the activities of the said Council and Committee and all
organs within its jurisdiction, organizations and enterprises on the territory
of Moscow. It is underlined that these measures are of a temporary nature
until the reasons for their complicity with the organizers of the state coup
are eliminated and clarified.

'1.1. By established procedures halt the carrying out of all banking operations receiving orders from organs, enterprises, and organizations of the said Council and Committee; sums entering the accounts of these organizations will be moved to the non-budget fund of social protection in Moscow.

'1.2. Vacate the premises, occupied by these organizations, organs and enterprises of the said Council and Committee, seal them up and keep watch over them (N. S. Myrikov).

'2. Request the Moscow Procurator to bring criminal proceedings against those officials, as well as other individuals that took part in illegal activities of supporting anticonstitutional organs.

'3. Request the Moscow Procurator to examine the decisions of organs of power on registration of charters (rules) of public organizations and other organizations and bring protests against the decision on registration of this or that, which established illegal links with the anticonstitutional organs.

'4. Measures taken in accordance with this order in relation to public organizations, their organs and officials, taking part in illegal activities, must not influence the limitation of rights and privileges, established by existing laws for veterans of war and labour. The government of Moscow, independently, in the shortest possible time will introduce into existence the procedure with which all organizational work for the realization of said privileges (the compiling of lists, the distribution of orders, the registration of veterans' certificates etc.) will be conducted by organs controlled by the government or the executive committee of local Soviets.

*Mayor of Moscow G. Popov''*

### 23.18. DECREE OF THE PRESIDENT OF THE REPUBLIC OF MOLDOVA

KISHINEV (RIA). Taking into account the difficult situation in the republic in connection with the illegal seizure of power in the USSR by the self-proclaimed State Emergency Committee, the President of Moldova, Mircha Snegur issued a Decree on Aug. 20 on the creation of a Higher Republican Council of Security, informs the Moldova-Press agency. This organ is called upon to govern the protection of essential services in the republic from possible encroachment by the armed forces and supporters of the State Emergency Committee, coordinate the actions of people who are ready to defend democratic struggles.

### 23.20. NOVOSIBIRSK: THE SITUATION IS CALM

NOVOSIBIRSK (RIA). The situation in Novosibirsk and the region is calm. At a session of the city Soviet, its chairman, Ivan Indinok, stressed that he had made his choice in favour of Russia. The chairman of the regional

Soviet, Vitali Mukha, made a speech on the local television and radio information services with a similar statement. Today, the presidium of the regional Soviet passed a resolution, in which this organ's adherence to Russian laws was officially set.

Meanwhile, the presidium of the regional Soviet called on the inhabitants of Novosibirsk Region not to support the carrying out of indefinite strikes.

According to the radio information programme, Mikroforum, in the Novosibirsk regional departments of the Interior and KGB, totally different orders are being given, which is putting the officials of these organizations in an uncertain situation.

## 23.31. STATEMENT OF THE COUNCIL OF THE ASSOCIATION OF SIBERIAN AND FAR-EASTERN CITIES

KHABAROVSK (RIA). The Council of the Association of Siberian and Far-Eastern Cities fully supports the RSFSR Supreme Soviet, the Russian President and government in their efforts to preserve on the territory of Russia legally elected organs of power. This is referred to in a statement by the Council. The Council calls upon the population of the cities of Siberia and the Far East and local Soviets to react against the striving of reactionary forces, and for the authorities of these cities to publicly express its attitude to events taking place by sending telegrams to the session of the Supreme Soviet of the Russian Federation.

## 23.42. VOLOGDA REGIONAL COUNCIL DOES NOT RECOGNIZE THE STATE EMERGENCY COMMITTEE

VOLOGDA (RIA). The presidium of the Vologda Regional Council of People's Deputies refuses to carry out any of the orders and statements of the State Emergency Committee. This is referred to in a resolution passed by the presidium.

## 23.45. KALININGRAD AUTHORITIES SUPPORT YELTSIN AND GORBACHEV

KALININGRAD (RIA). A state of emergency will not be introduced on the territory of Kaliningrad Region. This is referred to in an appeal by the presidium of the Regional Soviet of People's Deputies to the population of the region. On the evening of Aug. 20, on the central square of Kaliningrad, a large meeting gathered in support of the Russian leadership and the USSR President Gorbachev.

OMSK (PF). Late in the evening there was a meeting of the buro of the Omsk City Committee of the CPSU. The party leadership of Russia and the Union, who remained silent and did not give their assessment of the situation were condemned. The buro of the CPSU city committee demanded the calling before Aug. 26 of the plenums of the Central Committee of the

Russian Communist Party and the Central Committee of the CPSU, as well as the convocation of extraordinary congresses of the RSFSR and USSR Supreme Soviets, urgent information about the state of health of Mikhail Gorbachev and a speech by him on television and the radio. (Rossiiskaya gazeta, Aug. 23)

KHABAROVSK. The chairman of the Territorial Executive Committee, Vyacheslav Litvinov, announced that there was no state of emergency in the territory. Nobody had cancelled any of the RSFSR laws, they were valid. The head of the Department of the Interior of Khabarovsk territorial executive committee, V. Balanov, said: "We are subordinate to the decrees of the Russian President elected by the people. We feel that in the next few days, sessions of the Supreme Soviets of the USSR and Russian Federation will have the final say." (Rossiiskaya gazeta, Aug. 23)

YAKUTSK (PF). The Supreme Soviet and Council of Ministers of the republic declare adherence to the sovereignty proclaimed by the republic in September 1990 and in the future will be governed only by the Constitution of Yakutia. (Rossiiskaya gazeta, Aug. 23)

STAVROPOL (PF). The presidium of the Stavropol Territorial Soviet of People's Deputies came out with an appeal to the Supreme Soviet of the USSR, in which it insisted upon a speech by Mikhail Gorbachev on television. (Rossiiskaya gazeta, Aug. 23)

VLADIVOSTOK (PF). 115 deputies of the City Soviet (190 deputies in all) passed a resolution sharply condemning the seizure of power in the country by the State Emergency Committee, as well as demanding the immediate calling of an extraordinary congress of people's deputies of the USSR and RSFSR and the unblocking of banned sections of the media. The deputies stated the necessity of carrying out the decrees and orders of the legally elected authorities of Russia. (Rossiiskaya gazeta, Aug. 23)

KURGAN (PF). On Aug. 20 a joint meeting was held of Kurgan Regional Soviet and the regional executive committee, at which a resolution was passed on the implementation of the laws of the Russian Federation. The statement also mentions that no special measures will be taken and that the inhabi-tants of the region are asked to remain calm.

# AUGUST 21ST, 1991

167-188
00.07. RUSSIAN "WHITE HOUSE" UNDER ATTACK

Moscow (RIA). A column of armoured assault vehicles have approached the barricades around the parliament building from the direction of the US Embassy. People tried to stop the leading vehicle and the soldiers fired live cartridges into the air. The leading vehicles broke through the human chain by the US Embassy and are now moving towards the Novy Arbat (Prospekt Kalinina). At 00.05 Aug. 21 some 20 armoured vehicles broke through the first barricades on the New Arbat and headed in the direction of the parliament building.

00.25. WHITE HOUSE UNDER ATTACK: DEPUTIES ARE TRYING TO FIND WAYS TO INFLUENCE THE SOLDIERS

MOSCOW (RIA). At 00.20, Aug. 21 Russian Deputies held a short meeting in the offices of the Russian Information Agency in the parliament building. They discussed routes by which they could get out to meet the military units now concentrated around the White House. Krymsky Val and the Novy Arbat were described as particularly dangerous areas.

00.31. WHITE HOUSE UNDER ATTACK: FIRST CASUALTIES

MOSCOW (RIA). Single shots have been heard near the barricades across Smolenskaya Square. Picketers managed to cover the observation slits on one of the armoured assault vehicles with tarpaulin forcing it back into the tunnel under the Novy Arbat. Correspondents approached the cordon and one of them was called over by a major from the 27th brigade, who declined to give his name. This major informed RIA correspondents that the Russian parliament building would be stormed that night. 30 tanks and 40 armoured personnel carriers had been assigned to this operation which would involve approximately one thousand men. Armoured columns were at that moment moving from Tyoply Stan along Leninsky Prospekt. Several minutes ago a young man was shot at point blank range while trying to open the hatch of an armoured assault vehicle. His body was dragged behind the moving vehicle. Many of those forming the cordons have received cuts and injuries, some have been wounded.

According to eye-witness reports, trolleybusses barricading the Novy Arbat have been set on fire. APCs are continuing to clear the way towards the parliament building. Those manning the defences around the parliament building have sent out an appeal to the citizens of Russia and to Muscovites: "ALL TO THE WHITE HOUSE!"

00.35. RADIO STATION ECHO OF MOSCOW ONCE MORE CEASES BROADCASTING

MOSCOW (RIA). At 23.00, Aug. 20 the radio station Echo of Moscow once more went off the air. The Moscow OMON is now in the radio station and paratroopers are guarding it outside. According to the staff of Echo of Moscow, the "guards" are treating them well. Because of the introduction of a curfew in the capital the headquarters for emergency situation of the Moscow City Soviet advised staff to remain in the radio station building until morning.

MOSCOW (RF). According to unconfirmed reports coming from the Czechoslovak Embassy Jan Rybar, a journalist on the staff of the Czech newspaper Studenske Listy, has been wounded in the head near the parliament building. Rybar was taken to hospital, but his life is not thought to be in danger.

00.37. PUBLIC OPINION POLL IN VORONEZH

VORONEZH (RIA). 49 per cent of 724 people taking part in a public opinion poll declared that they believed the actions of the Emergency Committee to be illegal. 28 per cent believed that they were legal and 23 per cent don't-knows. Asked if they thought that the coming to power of the Emergency Committee would mean an improvement or a worsening of the economic situation in the country, 24 per cent replied that it would result in a worsening, but 38 per cent thought it would lead to an improvement. 37 per cent did not know.

57 per cent thought it likely that there would be mass repressions, 26 per cent thought it unlikely and 17 per cent said they didn't know.

00.38. BORIS GIDASPOV DID NOT KNOW THAT HE HAD BEEN INCLUDED IN THE LENINGRAD EMERGENCY COMMITTEE

LENINGRAD (RIA). "I did not know that I had been made a member of the Leningrad Emergency Committee, headed by Col.-Gen. Samsonov," declared Boris Gidaspov, First Secretary of the Leningrad Region Committee of the CPSU, in a speech on television, "but I believe that my appointment is quite normal, since I am a member of the Military Council of the Leningrad Military District".

## 01.03. ALEXANDER RUTSKOI ORDERS THE DEFENCE TO OPEN FIRE ON THE ATTACKERS

MOSCOW (RIA). In radio broadcast from the Supreme Soviet of the RSFSR Alexander Rutskoi, the Vice-President of Russia, appealed to the defenders of the parliament building. To avoid bloodshed and unnecessary casualties he called upon citizens to move back fifty metres from the parliament building and not to engage in clashes with the military.

Rutskoi also warned of a possible attempt on the building by KGB men in plainclothes. He ordered the parliament building defence forces to open fire on the attackers.

An armoured personnel carrier has been set on fire with a Molotov cocktail at the approaches to the Russian parliament building.

According to an RIA correspondent, units of the Kantemir Tank Division are approaching the White House from the direction of Kutuzovsky Prospekt. Officers have warned that they have been ordered to use live cartridges.

Information has just been received that units of the Caucasian Spetsnaz (special purpose forces) are moving along Kropotkinskaya Embankment.

Defence organizers at the White House are calling upon citizens gathered outsides to link hands and form a chain, and to use only methods of persuasion. According to information received, the soldiers of the Kantemir Division know nothing of what is really happening.

## 00.57. SAMARA OBEYS THE Russian PRESIDENT

SAMARA (RIA). On Aug. 20 a meeting of the presidium of the Regional Soviet of People's Deputies was held, at which a decision was taken to obey the Russian government and the President of the Russian Federation. A meeting was also held of the presidium of the City Soviet of People's Deputies, which adopted a similar decision.

An emergency session of the City Soviet was fixed for Aug. 21. The presidium of the Regional Soviet also decided that all decrees of the Russian President should be published in the regional newspapers and broadcast on local TV.

Yesterday evening (Aug. 20) the independent television company "Skad" broadcast the speech of Mayor of Leningrad Anatoli Sobchak.

01.30. FIRST ATTACK ON THE WHITE HOUSE BEATEN OFF
    MOSCOW (RIA). RIA on the spot corespondents' reports state that
the first attack on the White House has been beaten off. Unable to break
through the barricades of trolleybusses, the armoured personnel carriers
have retired to the Novy Arbat. Two of the defenders of the Russian
parliament have been killed near the US Embassy and several people have
been wounded. So far there has been no sight of any military manoeuvres
near the parliament building.
    Information has also been received that military units supported by
tanks are storming the Moscow City Soviet building, but there are no
reliable details on casualties and damage.

01.35. VITALI URAZHTSEV SAYS: "THE PLOTTERS ARE UNCER-
TAIN OF VICTORY."
    MOSCOW (RIA). Vitali Urazhtsev, President of the Schit Society
and Russian Deputy, told RIA reporters yesterday that he had been arrested
at 8.15 on the morning of August 19 as he stood at the bus stop near the
Comecon Building and taken to the HQ of the airborne troops.
    The officer in charge of the political department of the airborne
troops, Vladimir Polevik, and four other men--obviously agents of the
KGB--questioned him as to whether the Schit Society would take part in
armed resistance against the Emergency Committee and suggested that he
come over to the side of the Emergency Committee. About 13.00 on the
same day Urazhtsev received their apologies and was offered a car to take
him back.
    "We parted on very good terms. I believe that they are uncertain of
victory," he said. "They seem demoralized."

01.39. THE PEOPLE OF KRASNODAR SUPPORT THE Russian GOV-
ERNMENT
    KRASNODAR (RIA). Yesterday a well attended meeting was held
outside the territory executive committee building in Krasnodar in support
of the Russian government. Those attending declared that they would
continue to meet on the same spot each day.

01.45. ACTIONS OF THE COUP LEADERS CONDEMNED IN NOVO-
ROSSISK
    NOVOROSSIISK (RIA). At a well-attended meeting yesterday in
Novorossilsk, held with the agreement of the law-enforcing bodie, the
actions of the coup leaders were harshly condemned. There were calls for
the Emergency Committee and Yanayev in particular to be put on trial.
Many people signed an appeal in support of Yeltsin. Deputies from the City
Soviet speaking at the meeting condemned the Emergency Committee and

the presidium of the Novorossisk City Soviet who voted against the calling of an extraordinary session of the Soviet to give a political assessment of the situation. The deputies, however, are still hopeful that the session will be called. On Aug. 19 all portraits of Gorbachev disappeared from the building of the Novorossiisk City Executive Committee.

The strike committee of the Krasny Dvigatel Factory in Novorossiisk gave its full support to the Russian government and appealed to factory workers to condemn the actions of the Emergency Committee. A decision on whether to strike or for the moment issue a warning will be taken later this evening, Aug. 21.

01.49. APPEAL OF ALEXEI II, PATRIARCH OF ALL RUSSIA
MOSCOW (RIA). Brothers and Sisters!

The fragile peace in our society has been broken. Reports are coming in of the beginning of armed conflict and bloodshed.

In these times my duty as patriarch is to issue a warning to all those for whom the word of the Church is dear and not indifferent: whosoever takes up arms against his neighbour, against unarmed people, shall take a great sin upon his soul, excommunicating him from the Church and from God. For such more tears should be shed and more prayers uttered than for those who suffer at their hands. May the Lord protect us from the terrible sin of fratricide!

Therefore, I warn all fellow-countrymen. The Church will not bless, nor can it ever give its blessing to actions that are outside the law, violent and bloody.

I beg you all, dear brothers and sisters, to do everything in your power to prevent the flames of internecine war. Stop now!

I call upon the soldiers and their commanding officers to remember that the price of a human life is something that no one can state and no one can pay for.

In these days of the Fast of the Assumption I pray that the Holy Mother of God, the Protectress of our city, keep us under Her protection and preserve us all. Holy Mother of God, help us to be reconciled with each other, with he truth and with God.

*Alexei II, Patriarch of Moscow and All Russia*
*August 21, 1991. 1.30 a.m*

02.10. OFFICERS OF THE VOLGA-URALS MILITARY DISTRICT SUPPORT BORIS YELTSIN
SAMARA REGION (RIA). The press centres of the district Soviets in the town of Togliatti are handing out an appeal from the Volga-Urals military district to the citizens of Russia, signed by "Officers, loyal to their

oath''. The appeal refers to the events of August 19 as the usurpation of power. The appeal is addressed to Russian officers and calls upon them not to take up arms against the people and to remain loyal to their oath, to Russia and to President Yeltsin.

### 03.01. THE WHITE HOUSE UNDER ATTACK: THE SOLDIERS DO NOT INTEND TO SHOOT AT THE PEOPLE

MOSCOW (RIA). The situation on the square in front of the White House remains without change. The defence organizers have informed the crowds through loudspeakers that the soldiers of one of the military units have assured the Russian Deputies that they will not shoot at the people. An APC has been set on fire near the tunnel under the Novy Arbat. Chains of defenders are carrying out continual manoeuvres as information is received on the movements of the coup leaders' forces.

At 2.30 a group of rockers on motor-cycles returned from Kutuzovsky Prospekt to inform the defenders that no troops were to be seen on the Prospekt.

Rumours are circulating among the defenders of the parliament building that the Pskov Airborne Division has landed at Kubinka airport near Moscow and is at present advancing towards the city, but there has so far been no confirmation of these rumours.

### 03.04. MILITARY ASSURANCES THAT NO STORMING OF THE WHITE HOUSE IS CONTEMPLATED

MOSCOW (RIA). In a telephone conversation with USSR Deputy Volkov, the Deputy Defence Minister of the USSR, Col.-Gen. Vladislav Achalov, gave assurances that the storming of the White House was not part of the military high command's plans.

### 03.08. TSAREGORODTSEV CLAIMS EMERGENCY COMMITTEE LEADERSHIP HAS SWORN TO STOP THE TROOPS

MOSCOW (RIA). The head of the Secretariat of the Vice-President of the RSFSR, Alexei Tsaregorodtsev, told RIA corespondents:

"Over the last 1,1/2-2 hours our leaders have been in frequent contact with Yanayev, Moisseyev and Kalinin, commander of the Moscow Military District. They have also spoken to Lukyanov. Only Kryuchkov has been unavailable. All have sworn that they will stop the troops. At present it is quiet outside (i.e. outside the parliament building) and there are no rumblings. But how they intend to keep their word is something that is as yet difficult to say.''

### 03.21. MOSCOW CITY SOVIET: ATTACK UNLIKELY

MOSCOW (RIA). At 02.30 an RIA correspondent was informed at the Moscow City Soviet that there had been no attempt to storm the building. Columns of armoured vehicles had periodically passed the building moving in the direction of Pushkin Square.

### 03.24. INFANTRY ASSAULT VEHICLES SET ALIGHT: NO ONE CLAIMS OWNERSHIP

MOSCOW (RIA). The Deputy Minister of Internal Affairs of the USSR Col.-Gen. Boris Gromov denies categorically that the three infantry assault vehicles left burning at the approaches to the Russian parliament building belong to the Interior Ministry. Gromov informed members of the HQ for emergency situation of the Moscow City Soviet that he knew nothing of any losses inflicted on vehicles belonging to Interior Ministry troops.

The KGB department responsible for Moscow and the Moscow Region and the HQ of the Moscow military district similarly disclaim ownership of these vehicles.

It is assumed that the crews of these vehicles have suffered casualties.

### 03.42. THE STATE OF EMERGENCY, MOSCOW: TROOPS LEAVE THE CITY

MOSCOW (RIA). The General Director of the Mayor's Office, Yevgeni Sevastyanov informed the Russian Information Agency at 03.15 by telephone that at the present moment troops are leaving the city. He pointed out that his office had information on troop movements throughout the city.

Sevastyanov went on to say that from all appearances the troops had no precise time-table or deployment routes around the city. For this reason they were moving in a certain amount of disorder. But on the whole appeared to be leaving the city, and if they were unhampered they would leave quietly. Unfortunately, tragic misunderstandings were not to be excluded in those circumstances, where barricades and pickets had been previously erected in the path of the armoured columns. And this is just what happened at Smolenskaya Square, where the defenders of the Russian parliament clashed with troops. As a result there were casualties.

Information received from GAI (traffic police) posts around the city and other reports coming into the mayor's office over the last couple of hours, said Yevgeni Sevastyanov, suggest that the armoured columns are crossing the outer ring road in one direction only--away from Moscow.

OMSK (PF). Information received from sources close to the local KGB state that at 4 a.m. a coded message was received from Gennadi Yanayev ordering a state of emergency to be declared in Omsk. This was discussed by city and regional leaders. It is assumed that this meeting was presided over by Ivan Nazarov, First Secretary of the Regional Committee of the CPSU. The chairman of the local television and radio committee declared that only information received from the All Russia Teleradio Network would be broadcast. Yeltsin's decree assuming the powers of Supreme Commander-in-Chief was not broadcast by the Omsk television and radio committee.

04.16. THE CHIEF OF STAFF OF THE MOSCOW MILITARY DIS-TRICT STATES THAT THE WITHDRAWAL OF TROOPS FROM THE CITY IS GOING AHEAD AT FULL SPEED
MOSCOW (RIA). The Chief of Staff of the Moscow Military District Lt.-Gen. Leonid Zolotov has told deputies of the Moscow City Soviet that the withdrawal of troops from the city is going ahead at full speed. By 03.30 Moscow time the Taman Division had already been withdrawn and the Kantemir Tank Division was preparing for withdrawal. He stated also that he knew nothing of the movements of the other tank columns, unconfirmed reports of the presence of which are regularly being received from various places.

04.20. MOSCOW COMMANDANT BELIEVES THERE WILL BE NO STORMING OF THE WHITE HOUSE
MOSCOW (RIA). In an interview with an RIA correspondent the Military Commandant of Moscow, Lt.-Gen. Smirnov, expressed his deep regret over the loss of life. He stated that rumours about a "storming of the White House"' were "crude inventions, bordering on provocation". In his opinion there was no one among the military leadership who could give the order for attack, since this would entail bloodshed. He also added that the troops would not attempt to take the White House tomorrow either, or the day after.
Lt.-Gen. Smirnov described rumours about the landing of paratroopers at Kubinka as groundless and reports that the Kantemir Division was on Kutuzovsky Prospekt as provocation.

05.16. SEIZURE OF THE TELEVISION CENTRE IN TALLINN
TALLINN (RIA). At approximately 5 a.m. this morning a platoon of troops seized the first two stories of the telecentre in Estonia's capital, stated the ETA Agency. But staff at the telecentre succeeded in raising the lifts which held up further advancement.

06.07. INFANTRY ASSAULT VEHICLES WITHDRAWN FROM THE CONFLICT ZONE
MOSCOW (RIA). Intervention by Russian Deputies, particularly Gleb Yakunin and Vladimir Kryuchkov (not to be confused with the KGB

Chairman), early this morning helped six infantry assault vehicles and their crews that had been surrounded by incensed crowds near Smolenskaya Square withdraw from the conflict zone. These vehicles had been involved during the night in an accidental conflict between columns of the Kantemir Division leaving the city and Muscovites picketing the approaches to the parliament building.

This tragic incident, which involved loss of life was mistakenly understood as the beginning of an attack on the White House.

After Russian Deputies had spoken to both sides involved in the conflict, all the infantry assault vehicles were withdrawn from the conflict zone and now under the Russian flag moved off in the direction of the White House. It is believed that their crews will now join the parliament building defence force.

07.42. PARATROOPS FROM ODESSA AT THE "GATES" OF MOS-COW.

MOSCOW (RIA). The early morning of August 21 has virtually seen the withdrawal from the City of Moscow of the troops sent in on August 19 as a result of the declaration of a state of emergency. At the same time a column of fifty or more armoured assault vehicles of one of the regiments of the Balgrad Airborne Division has this morning been seen advancing on Moscow. The column is now standing at the intersection of the Mozhaiskoye Shosse and the Moscow outer ring road--the city's official boundary.

The paratroopers, who include many veterans of the Afghan War, told RIA correspondents that they were only told where they were flying once they had boarded the plane. Before take off from Odessa--where the division is permanently deployed--the soldiers were ordered not to shoot and not to give in to provocation. They gave assurances that they would only use their weapons if fired upon.

The soldiers could not say with any certainty whether their regiment was the vanguard of the Balgrad Division, or whether they had any specific objective.

Units of this division have previously been sent to Baku and Yerevan to maintain law and order in these cities.

10.21. THE LENINGRAD CITY AND REGIONAL SOVIETS SUPPORT THE ACTIONS OF THE SUPREME SOVIET OF THE RSFSR AND THE RUSSIAN PRESIDENT

LENINGRAD (RIA). At a joint extraordinary session of the Lenin-grad City and Regional Soviets support was expressed for the actions of the Supreme Soviet and the President of Russia aimed at assuming full powers throughout the republic until legal union power could be restored. Enter-prises and institutions in the city and in the Leningrad Region were advised to be guided by the Constitution and laws of the USSR and the RSFSR as well as by the decrees and orders issued by the Russian President and the Mayor of Leningrad. The commander-in-chief of the Leningrad Military District was asked to repudiate the communique on the introduction of a state of emergency in the city and dissolve the emergency commission. To coordinate action in the present situation a permanent headquarters was formed of the Mayor, Anatoli Sobchak, members of the presidiums of the Leningrad City and Regional Soviets and a number of People's Deputies.

## 10.28. LATVIA: THE PREVIOUS NIGHT'S DEVELOPMENTS--AN ASSESSMENT

RIGA (RIA). During the previous night the commander-in-chief of the Baltic Military District Col.-Gen. Fyodor Kuzmin, who supports the line of the Emergency Committee in the Baltic States, rang the Chairman of the Latvian Council of Ministers Ivar Godmanis and warned that he was sending two armoured personnel carriers to the Council of Ministers building in order to remove superfluous arms from those guarding the building. Arriving in the uniforms of paratroops, the soldiers disarmed the guards on the ground floor. Several persons including Andris Bunka, a security aide to the prime-minister, and an officer of the guard were escorted away to an unknown destination. But when later representatives of the military district command, headed by Gen. Dudkin, arrived to speak to Godmanis, they stated that the disarming of the building's guards had been carried out by unknown persons without the knowledge of the military commanders.

## 10.43. THE MOSCOW CITY SOVIET AND THE MOSCOW REGIONAL SOVIET APPEAL TO CITIZENS TO DEFEND THE PARLIAMENT BUILDING

MOSCOW (RIA). The Moscow City and Regional Soviets have appealed to the inhabitants of Moscow and the suburbs to come to the Krasnopresnenskaya Embankment this evening to defend the White House. They have also asked for information on troop movements around the Moscow Region. The telephone number to contact is 299-33-51.

## 11.03. DECLARATION OF THE LEADERSHIP OF THE CENTRAL COMMITTEE OF THE KOMSOMOL

MOSCOW (RIA). The leadership of the Central Committee of the Komsomol has appealed to all the mass media "in view of the closing down of the newspaper Komsomolskaya Pravda" to publish its declaration. The latter states that there are no grounds for recognizing the constitutional character of the measures taken in the name of the "Soviet leadership" or their compliance with the letter of the Law of the USSR "On the Legal

Introduction of a State of Emergency''. The declaration also considers that the explanation given by the Emergency Committee for the removal of the President of the USSR is unconvincing.

The Central Committee of the Komsomol demands the immediate convening of the Congress of People's Deputies and that Mikhail Gorbachev should be given the opportunity to speak to the people.

"We have special words for the soldiers, most of whom are young men," states the declaration. "We believe that under no circumstances should you stain your honour and consciences by spilling the blood of your fellow-countrymen."

11.09. MOSCOW (RIA). DECREE NO. 65 OF THE PRESIDENT OF THE RSFSR: ON ENSURING THE FUNCTIONING OF ENTERPRISES AND ORGANIZATIONS IN THE RSFSR

The negotiations held on August 20, 1991 between the leadership of the RSFSR and the Chairman of the Supreme Soviet of the USSR Comrade Lukyanov who has to all intents and purposes distanced himself from the so-called State Committee for the State of Emergency of the USSR, confirm the unconstitutional character of the formation and actions of this committee. With regard for the results of the negotiations and the fact that both the Supreme Soviet of the USSR and the Supreme Soviet of the RSFSR will consider the actions of the State Committee for the State of Emergency of the USSR illegal, I decree the following:

1. The directors of all enterprises and organizations located on the territory of the RSFSR, irrespective of the ministries and departments they come under and the form of their property, should ensure the normal running of their enterprises and organizations in accordance with the laws of the RSFSR and the USSR until special instructions from the leadership of the RSFSR.

2. Any decisions or enactments of the State Committee for the State of Emergency or any other bodies acting on its instructions on economic matters be banned on the territory of the RSFSR.

3. In accordance with the Law of the RSFSR "On Enterprises and Entrepreneurial Activity" the labour collectives at enterprises and organizations should give assistance to the directors in carrying out this Decree. President of the RSFSR, Boris Yeltsin

*Moscow, Kremlin*
*August 20, 1991*

11.31. TANK DETACHMENT HAS QUIT ITS POST OUTSIDE THE NOVOSTI INFORMATION AGENCY OFFICES

MOSCOW (RIA). 7 tanks, 2 APCs and a command car quit their post at 11.00 this morning after spending two days and nights "guarding" the offices of the Novosti Information Agency

11.22. DECLARATION OF THE KARABAKH COMMITTEE OF THE RUSSIAN INTELLIGENTSIA

MOSCOW (RIA). The Moscow branch of the Karabakh Committee of the Russian Intelligentsia has issued a declaration stating that as a result of the onslaught against democracy there is an increasing possibility of a worsening of the situation in Nagorny Karabakh and that there is a threat to the on-going process of democratization in Armenia. The committee calls upon public organizations in Armenia and Nagorny Karabakh to condemn the unconstitutional actions of the Emergency Committee and express solidarity with the democratic forces of Russia.

11.30. EXTRAORDINARY SESSION OF THE SUPREME SOVIET OF RUSSIA

MOSCOW (RIA). An extraordinary session of the Supreme Soviet of the RSFSR opened this morning in the parliament building in Moscow. Only one question is on the agenda: ''The Political Situation in the RSFSR as a result of the Coup d'Etat.''

11.35. RUSLAN KHASBULATOV ON THE SITUATION IN THE COUNTRY

MOSCOW (RIA). Opening the session of parliament, Ruslan Khasbulatov stated: ''An extraordinary session of the Supreme Soviet of Russia has been called in these tragic days for the Motherland.'' He emphasized that the country had experienced an ''unconstitutional coup'' and that its organizers had ''brought the country to the brink of civil war''. Khasbulatov noted that the Russian people had countered this with their ''will and resolution''. He expressed admiration for the fortitude of the people of Moscow, who had come to the defence of the President, the Parliament and the Russian Government. He also singled out the position of the leaders of Kazakhstan, the Ukraine, the Caucasian Republics and Moldova noting only that their reaction had been a little belated. He also referred to the firm position taken by the Western leaders and the heads of state of Eastern Europe. He said that earlier that morning Boris Yeltsin had had a telephone conversation with President Mitterrand of France, who spoke of the legality of the actions of the Russian leadership.

11.50. THE SOYUZ FACTION FIRST SUPPORTED THE COUP, NOW IT IS ''ASSESSING DEVELOPMENTS''

MOSCOW (RIA). On August 19 a member of the presidium of the Soyuz faction, Georgi Tikhonov gave unconditional support in the name of that faction of the union parliament for the actions of the Emergency Committee. Earlier this morning an RIA correspondent telephones the co-chairman of the Soyuz faction Yuri Blokhin and asked for his assessment of the situation at present, after the first casualties had occurred during the previous night. Blokhin said: "We are assessing and reviewing developments, since the situation is far from simple and events are turning our differently from the way that was thought previously. Our group insisted on the introduction of a state of emergency by constitutional means at the Congress of People's Deputies of the USSR."

11.56.
MOSCOW (RIA). Declaration of the government of Moscow:
By order of the Commandant of the Moscow Military District, Col.-Gen. Kalinin a curfew was imposed in Moscow on Aug. 20.

The government of Moscow considers it necessary to state the following:

The situation in the city as a whole and the criminal situation in particular are fully under the control of the city authorities. The only destabilizing factor is the actions of the unconstitutional Emergency Committee. The presence in the city of a large number of troops and armoured vehicles has hampered the distribution of food to the shops as well as the work of the postal and ambulance services and road repair and other work. Furthermore, roads that have only recently been repaired and resurfaced are being spoilt and the environment is suffering.

The presence of troops and armoured vehicles in the city and their manoeuvring around the streets damages the normal life of the capital. It represents a permanent danger to the population, increases tension and could provoke disorders.

Despite the high self-discipline and restraint of the people of Moscow and the selfless actions of the deputies and the organs of executive power, the irresponsible actions of the self-appointed State Emergency Committee have resulted in loss of life.

Realizing our responsibility for the fate of the inhabitants of Moscow and acting on behalf of the mandate we received as the result of free elections, we declare the introduction of a curfew illegal, and demand its lifting and the immediate withdrawal of troops from the city.

*Yuri Luzhkov*
*Vice-Mayor and Premier of the Government of Moscow*
*August 21, 1991*

12.00. NO OFFICIAL INFORMATION ON THE NUMBER OF CASUALTIES IN MOSCOW
MOSCOW (RIA). There is still no proper information on the number of casualties in the clashes between soldiers and demonstrators at the intersection of the Sadovoye Ring Road and New Arbat. Hospitals, including the Sklifasovsky Emergency Hospital, and the Main Moscow Medical

Directorate say they "do not possess" this information. The duty officer at the Chief Administration of the Interior for Moscow repeated the information given by the national television that two men were run over by a tank. Sources close to the Russian White House say "two, three or four people were crushed to death by an infantry assault vehicle" and "one or two were killed by gunfire".

NORILSK (PF). The Taimyr regional branch of the Russian Democratic Party appealed to the people to support the position of the Russian leadership. The paper Zapolyarnaya pravda came out in support of the City Committee of the CPSU, which called upon the people of Norilsk to work normally so as to stabilize the situation.

NOVGOROD (PF). A session of the City Soviet passed a resolution not to obey the enactments and decrees of the self-styled State Emergency Committee, and be guided only by the legal acts of the Parliament and government of Russia. The formation of the Emergency Committee is looked upon as a fascist coup.

BRYANSK (PF). The chairman of the Regional Soviet, A.N. Veselov, announced on the radio that he remains loyal to the Constitution of Russia. The presidium of the Regional Soviet made an appeal to the people, which among other things stated that the legally elected organs would continue to function throughout the Bryansk Region.

BLAGOVESCHENSK (PF). At a meeting of the executive committee of the democratic bloc "For the Renewal of Russia" a declaration by a group of deputies was adopted, which said: "An unconstitutional coup has taken place in Moscow. The ousting of the president of the country is an illegal act."

SARATOV (PF). The editors of the City Soviet newspaper Saratov came out unconditionally in support of the constitutional authorities of the republic. The chief editor, Boris Plokhotenko, told our correspondent: "Let it be our last issue, but we will not act against our consciences--the people of Saratov will know the truth about the coup."

## 12.09. APPEAL FROM ALL-UNION COUNCIL OF SOLDIERS' PARENTS

MOSCOW (RIA). The All-Union Council of Soldiers' Parents expressed their full support for the Appeal of the Russian Leadership, condemned the formation of the State Emergency Committee and demanded that the President of the USSR, Mikhail Gorbachev, be given the opportunity to speak on national television. They insisted on the immediate calling of an emergency Congress of People's Deputies of the USSR. They also called upon the people of the country to begin an indefinite general strike.

At present members of the All-Union Council of Soldiers' Parents are making their way to the military units to persuade the soldiers "not to take part in the coup".

## 12.16. ECHO OF MOSCOW TRANSMISSION SWITCHED OFF ON ORDERS OF THE CITY COMMANDANT

MOSCOW (RIA). According to Sergei Fonton, assistant editor-in-chief of Echo of Moscow, "the radio station was switched off the air at 10.18 this morning on the orders of a group of paratroopers, who forced their way into the station. According to the commanding officer of the group, Lt. Col. Zakharov, this was done on the orders of the city commandant. The reason was due to an unknown radio station which broadcast from 01.19 to 03.47 on our wavelength and with our signature tunes. For two and a half hours the provocateurs broadcast false information, sharply exaggerating the number of casualties."

## 12.30. MILITARY SEIZE TV AND RADIO STATIONS

VILNIUS (RIA). At approximately 04.00 this morning Soviet Army soldiers occupied TV and radio stations in the towns of Siauliai, Viesinta and Panevezys, according to the Lithuanian Information Bureau. Staff in the buildings were forced out. In Panevezys a local telephone exchange was also seized.

## 12.55. RUSSIAN SUPREME SOVIET AWAITS ARRIVAL OF KRYUCHKOV

MOSCOW (RIA). KGB Chairman Vladimir Kryuchkov is to appear at the extraordinary session of the Supreme Soviet of the Russian Federation at 13.00 Moscow time. This was reported at the session, which opened earlier this morning, by Russian President Boris Yeltsin.

## 13.10. YELTSIN'S SPEECH TO THE EXTRAORDINARY SESSION OF THE SUPREME SOVIET OF THE RUSSIAN FEDERATION

MOSCOW (RIA). "The coup," said Boris Yeltsin, speaking at an extraordinary session of the Russian parliament, "took place exactly at the time when democracy was beginning to grow and gather pace." He reminded deputies that there had already been two previous attempts at a right-wing coup--at the end of 1990, which was only stopped by the statement of Eduard Shevardnadze and the attitude taken by the rest of the world, and at a recent session of the Supreme Soviet of the USSR, "when those same persons who organized the present coup demanded special powers for themselves".

Yeltsin stated again that the coup was "unconstitutional, as there had been no statements from the legally elected president of the country, nor any medical evidence produced that Gorbachev was unable to work". He referred to the opinion of the President's personal doctor, who had seen Gorbachev on the eve of the coup.

Yeltsin reported his conversations on the telephone with the leaders of the Western countries and the Union republics, who in his words told him that they strongly condemned the "unconstitutional coup, that they would not recognize the State Emergency Committee and that they would continue to support the Russian leadership". He said further that they would take all steps to ensure that the rest of the world expressed its attitude to the events in the USSR. Yeltsin requested that the Western leaders demand contact with President Gorbachev, isolated in his dacha in the Crimea.

13.20. RUSLAN KHASBULATOV ON THE REASONS FOR THE COUP
MOSCOW (RIA). "The unconstitutional coup was mounted in a bid to torpedo the new Union Treaty," said Ruslan Khasbulatov, acting chairman of the Russian parliament, in a speech this morning to the extraordinary session of the Supreme Soviet of the Russian Republic. Another "reason for the coup", he said, was discontent among reactionary forces with the influence of the progressive policies of the Russian leadership on developments in the country. One of the "main aims of the conspirators", Khasbulatov said, was to get rid of the Russian leadership. The coup was a reaction to the policy of radical reforms, which after long hesitation the President of the USSR, Mikhail Gorbachev, had adopted.

Khasbulatov called upon the parliamentarians to adopt at the session a package of resolutions, particularly, a law approving the actions of the President of Russia, Boris Yeltsin. He said he believed that at such a decisive moment differences between the members of the Supreme Soviet should be forgotten.

The parliamentary leader expressed his indignation at the way recent events in the country had been presented in Pravda, Sovetskaya Rossiya and on Soviet television. He proposed that these information services should be immediately nationalized at the present session. He also said he was surprised at the stand taken by correspondents on these media services, who put up with directors who were "ready to work in the service of any authority".

13.31. SESSION AUTHORIZES SILAYEV TO MEET GORBACHEV, KRYUCHKOV NOT COMING TO PARLIAMENTARY SESSION
MOSCOW (RIA). "We need to be certain that Gorbachev is alive and well," said Russian Prime Minister Ivan Silayev at the extraordinary session of the Russian parliament. He asked the deputies to authorize himself and the Russian Vice-President, Alexander Rutskoi to fly out with

KGB Chairman, Vladimir Kryuchkov, and a team of medical experts to the place where President Gorbachev was being confined. This suggestion was adopted unanimously.

One of the deputies (name at present unknown to the RIA) stated that he had positive information that Kryuchkov had ordered the Spetsnaz (special-purpose unit) of the KGB and the General Staff Chief Intelligence Administration to effect a seizure of the Moscow White House and intern the Russian leadership. But Khasbulatov demanded proof of this and interrupted the deputy's report. A break of 30 minutes was declared and in that time the report came in that Kryuchkov would not be coming to the session.

13.53. YELTSIN SAYS MEMBERS OF STATE EMERGENCY COM-
MITTEE ON THEIR WAY TO AIRPORT
    MOSCOW (RIA). Russian President Boris Yeltsin has just informed the extraordinary session of the Supreme Soviet that "members of the so-called State Emergency Committee are on their way to Vnukovo Airport". He proposed authorizing Aeroflot, the Russian KGB and the Russian Interior Ministry to detain them at the airport. This proposal was approved. Eye witnesses told RIA corespondents that two limousines belonging to KGB chief Vladimir Kryuchkov were in the inner courtyard of the KGB building being loaded with baggage just before midday. They later departed for an unknown destination.

14.06. SVERDLOVSK OMON READY TO FLY TO MOSCOW TO
SUPPORT RUSSIAN GOVERNMENT
    MOSCOW (RIA). Sverdlovsk OMON has informed the Russian State Defence Committee that they are ready to fly to Moscow to support and defend the Russian parliament building. The Committee Chairman, Col. Gen. Kobets had previously sent a fax message to Sverdlovsk stating the need for this help.
    OMSK (PF). In a conversation with the Chairman of the City Soviet, Vladimir Varnavsky, commander of the Omsk garrison Lt. Gen. Moroz declared his loyalty to the Russian government. Moroz' reaction to Yeltsin's decree assuming the functions of Supreme Commander-in-Chief is not yet known. Members of the Omsk regional recruiting office are looking at local press centres to see who among the journalists are liable to be called up as reservists. The local daily newspapers, Vecherny Omsk and Omskaya pravda came out today without publishing the communiques and enactments of the Russian government, thereby disobeying yesterday's decree of the City Soviet. The weekly Oreol came out as Xerox copy in two special editions carrying information from the RIA and the IMA-press on the situation in the country, and the Decrees of the Russian president.

## 14.12. KGB DEMANDS AN END TO TELEVISING RUSSIAN PARLIAMENT SESSION

MOSCOW (RIA). Acting Chairman of the Russian Parliament, Ruslan Khasbulatov has reported that two KGB agents came to the parliament building and demanded that the televised broadcast of the session be ended.

## 14.20. TROOPS TO BE WITHDRAWN FROM CENTRE OF MOSCOW

MOSCOW (RIA). Agreement has been reached between Vice-Mayor Luzhkov and Chief of Staff of the Moscow Military District, Zolotov, on the withdrawal of troops from the central parts of the city and their concentration on two spots on the outskirts. This was reported at a meeting of the presidium of the Moscow City Soviet. Talks are continuing on the further withdrawal of troops from Moscow.

14.24. MOSCOW (RIA). RUSSIAN PRESIDENT BORIS YELTSIN APPEALS TO THE MEN OF THE DZERZHINSKY MOTORIZED INFANTRY DIVISION:

"Soldiers, Countrymen, Sons of Russia!

"I, President of Russia, elected by the will of our much-suffering nation, appeal to you at this time of tribulation for our country. A choice lies before you: either to aid and abet a group of conspirators and usurpers by obeying their criminal orders and thereby going against your own people, or to defend democracy and the nation's legally elected government.

"The former will embroil the country in fratricidal civil war and bloodshed; the latter will ensure peace, constitutional order and security.

"My dear sons! I am relying on you to make the right choice. I hope that you will come out on the side of the legal government, the Russian president. I am sure that you will not permit such bloodshed, nor give your fathers and mothers cause to weep bitter tears for their sons. Countrymen! Soldiers! Men of the Dzerzhinsky Division!

"I give you the following orders: immediately and without hesitation come over to the side of the legal government in an orderly and disciplined fashion.

"Great Russia, insulted and humiliated as she may be, calls out to you."

## 14.55. MEMBERS OF STATE EMERGENCY COMMITTEE THOUGHT TO HAVE QUIT MOSCOW

MOSCOW (RIA). An RIA correspondent reports that the presidential plane has just left Vnukovo-2 Airport. There are some grounds for believing that several members of the State Emergency Committee and persons close to them are on board and heading for the Crimea. Another plane left shortly afterwards for the same destination carrying Russian Prime Minister Ivan

Silayev. At the same time information has been received by RIA from an officer responsible for in-flight radio communications with the presidential plane, who wishes to remain anonymous. This officer said that at approximately 14.00 he was ordered by the KGB department for presidential communications to begin operating the satellite link-up. He also told RIA that on Aug. 19 he was supposed to have maintained communications during Gorbachev's flight from the Crimea to Moscow, but instead he received orders that the flight would not take place.

### 15.04. "I ABSOLUTELY REFUSE TO ACCEPT THE LAWLESSNESS THAT IS GOING ON IN THE COUNTRY", DECLARES VADIM BAKATIN

MOSCOW (RIA). "I absolutely refuse to accept the lawlessness that is going on in the country," said USSR presidential adviser Vadim Bakatin to the extraordinary session of the Russian parliament. "As both citizen and official member of the USSR Security Council, I am full of respect for the actions of the Russian leadership, the deputies and the citizens of Moscow."

Bakatin arrived at the session having learned of Kryuchkov's proposal that Yeltsin should fly together with him to see Gorbachev in the Crimea. Bakatin intended to propose that he should make the journey in Yeltsin's stead, believing that such a move would be too dangerous for the Russian President. He insisted that instead of Silayev or Rutskoi, he himself or Yevgeni Primakov should be sent.

Bakatin believes that the most pressing objective at present is for Gorbachev to be allowed to speak, since the main thing is not to give the USSR deputies the opportunity of giving the coup a constitutional character.

### 15.12. ARKADI VOLSKY HAS SPOKEN TO MIKHAIL GORBACHEV ON THE TELEPHONE

MOSCOW (RIA). Arkadi Volsky, Chairman of the Scientific Industrial Union (SIU) and one of the originators of the Movement for Democratic Reform, spoke on the telephone today with President Mikhail Gorbachev, who was removed from power on Aug. 19 by the conspirators and has been under house arrest in the Crimea since. Sources at SIU say that the President's health is good, but refused to give any more information until Volsky holds a press conference.

### 15.15. KRAVCHUK WARNS LUKYANOV AGAINST ANNOUNCING A STATE OF EMERGENCY IN THE UKRAINE

KIEV (RIA). Head of the Ukrainian parliament Leonid Kravchuk spoke earlier today on the telephone with the Chairman of the Supreme Soviet of the USSR, Anatoli Lukyanov. He gave a warning that if the state of emergency was introduced into the Ukraine there would be mass incidents of civil disobedience and added that he would not appeal to the people to refrain from taking part in them.

15.20. KALININ FACTORY DEMANDS RESIGNATION OF ITS GENERAL DIRECTOR AND STATE EMERGENCY COMMITTEE MEMBER, ALEXANDER TIZYAKOV
SVERDLOVSK (RIA). An extraordinary session of the Regional Soviet today supported Russian leaders' Appeal to the Citizens of Russia and declared that they would introduce a pre-strike situation throughout the region. The workers of the Kalinin Machine Tools Factory production association were asked to review the part played in the coup by its General Director, Alexander Tizyakov, as a member of the State Emergency Committee.

Workers from the 204th Shop of the Kalinin Factory appealed at a meeting to the rest of the factory employees to begin immediate amalgamation under the jurisdiction of Russia. The appeal also contained a demand that General Director Tizyakov be dismissed and prosecuted for his part in the coup. The appeal was supported at a meeting of the whole factory. A strike committee was formed and a decision taken to strike.

15.24. UKRAINIAN PARLIAMENTARY OPPOSITION DEMANDS AN EXTRAORDINARY SESSION OF THE SUPREME SOVIET OF THE REPUBLIC
KIEV (RIA). Earlier today a group of deputies from the Narodnaya Rada faction in the Ukrainian parliament met with Chairman Leonid Kravchuk and demanded that he call an extraordinary session of parliament. Protest was also made against the arrest of USSR President Mikhail Gorbachev on Ukrainian territory The Crimea is officially part of the Ukraine.by local Sebastopol KGB.

15.39. DECLARATION OF USSR SCIENTIFIC INDUSTRIAL UNION
MOSCOW (RIA). The Scientific Industrial Union of the USSR issued a declaration earlier today demanding that an emergency Congress of the USSR People's Deputies be called and Mikhail Gorbachev given the opportunity to speak at it. The declaration was signed by directors and managers from industrial unions, associations and amalgamations, banks, joint ventures and other leasing and cooperative enterprises. They pointed to the deleterious effects of the coup attempt on the economy, on democracy and on the maintenance of law and order.

15.42. ARMENIAN COMMISSIONS PROTEST OVER ARREST OF GDLYAN

YEREVAN (RIA). The judicial commission and the commission on human and national rights of the Armenian Supreme Soviet sent a demand to the Chairman of the Supreme Soviet of the USSR and the Prosecutor-General of the USSR for the release of Telman Gdlyan following his recent arrest. Expressing their concern for the fate of Deputy Gdlyan, the Armenian commissions condemned illegal acts of this nature and emphasized their incompatibility with the international obligations of the USSR in relation to legality and human rights.

15.44. RADIO RUSSIA ON THE AIR AGAIN

MOSCOW (RIA). At 2.30 this afternoon Radio Russia began broadcasting once again from the studio in Yamskoye Polye. Broadcasts can be heard on the 1100 metre band or 261 kilohertz medium wave.

15.52. MOSCOW HOSPITALS REPORT WOUNDED

MOSCOW (RIA). A duty doctor at the Pirogov Hospital has informed the RIA that a 51-year-old man was brought in the middle of the night from Smolenskaya Square. The doctor said "the nature of the wounds found on the chest, stomach and limbs suggest that they were caused by blank rounds fired from an automatic weapon at close range".

At 01.00 this morning (Aug. 21) a 32-year-old man was brought from the intersection of the Sadovoye Ring Road and New Arbat to Hospital No. 15 suffering from bullet wounds in the shoulder. The shots had been fired from an infantry assault vehicle and the wounded man did not see what weapon had been used.

16.14. MEMBERS OF STATE EMERGENCY COMMITTEE ARRESTED, YAZOV SHOOTS HIMSELF

MOSCOW (RIA). Unconfirmed reports claim that six members of the State Emergency Committee, who seized power early in the morning of Aug. 19, have been arrested. The same sources also report that Defence Minister Dmitri Yazov has committed suicide. The Chief of the General Staff has made himself acting defence minister. It is expected that he will shortly appear at the Russian parliament for talks.

16.41. THE SITUATION THROUGHOUT RUSSIA

MOSCOW (RIA). RIA correspondents report:

KRASNODAR. All newspapers have come out without any limitations imposed on them. Two local papers Sovetskaya Kuban and Kubanskiye novosti have published official material from the State Emergency Committee, while the youth paper Komsomolets Kubani has printed documents from the President and government of Russia.

VLADIVOSTOK. Forty tanks are deployed in the resort zone 30 kilometres from the city. Earlier today there was a meeting in support of Yeltsin on the central square. A group of deputies from the local Primorye Soviet announced the formation of a Coordinating Strike Committee, but called upon employees not to stop work until they had received special instructions from the Russian leadership. At the meeting citizens began being registered for the Russian National Guard.

SVERDLOVSK. Earlier today workers at the North Urals Bauxite Mine downed tools, as did other workers in the town of Berezovsky. In Sverdlovsk itself workers at Uralmash works, the Avtomatika factory, the Novator design and construction bureau and a rubber factory have also gone out on strike.

KEMEROVO. An extraordinary session of the Regional Soviet opened earlier today. Chairman Aman Tuleyev confirmed that the laws of the Russian republic would continue to be in force throughout the Kemerovo Region. All newspapers have come out and TV and radio stations are broadcasting. Reports from the regional Soviet state that 15 mines and 2 mining directorates are on strike. Forty worker collectives are also reported to be striking for political reasons.

VOLGOGRAD. The chairman of the Executive Committee of the Regional Soviet, Ivan Shabunin, said that in the event of the forcible removal of the legal organs of Soviet government, the extreme measures would be taken up to and including the calling of a general strike. But at another meeting of the directors of the town's major enterprises the call to strike was rejected, although those attending the meeting declared their support for the Russian government. A representative of the Volgograd Interior Department, speaking on television, said that the local police force would act in accordance with the orders and instructions of the Russian Interior Ministry.

KHABAROVSK. At a meeting attended by thousands citizens it was agreed to send a telegram to the Supreme Soviets of the USSR and Russia demanding the immediate arrest of the members of the State Emergency Committee and their prosecution. The presidium of the Khabarovsk Regional Soviet declared that it would not carry out the instructions of the State Emergency Committee.

MOSCOW. The presidium of the General Confederation of Trade Unions Council demanded that Mikhail Gorbachev speak to the people on national television. The Council leadership said that any use of force against the civilian population was inadmissible and insisted that there be a meeting of the USSR Supreme Soviet at the earliest possible moment.

YAKUTSK (PF). The Chairman of the Yakut-Sakha Supreme Soviet, Mikhail Nikolayev, declared the allegiance of the republican leadership to the Declaration of the Republic's State Sovereignty. The leadership did not believe there was any reason for the formation of emergency committees in Yakutia or for any other organs of the State Emergency Committee. "We declare," Nikolayev said, "that organs of Soviet power legally elected by the people function throughout the Yakut-Sakha Republic." He called upon the people to remain calm and restrained. (Rossiiskaya gazeta, August 23, 1991).

ULAN-UDE (PF). A meeting of Buryat leaders held in the presence of correspondents adopted a resolution to support the State Emergency Committee and to set up an emergency committee in the republic. Prime Minister Saganov asked the police to, in his words, "politely" clear the Soviet Square of those attending the rally. This rally was reported by the local papers. But a TV broadcast of the extraordinary session of the Russian parliament forced a sharp change of plans. According to Andrei Butyugov, a reporter for Pravda Buryatii, who was present at the meeting, the type was reset and the originals destroyed. In the morning the Republic of Buryatiya was unanimous in its support for democracy. (Rossiiskaya gazeta, August 23, 1991.)

KEMEROVO (PF). A group of 30 men from the emergency volunteer corps has set out from the mining town of Mezhdurechensk and is flying to Moscow to help guard the Russian parliament building.

## 16.56. STATE EMERGENCY COMMITTEE HAS MOVED TO THE CRIMEA

MOSCOW (RIA). Ruslan Khasbulatov has stated at the extraordinary session of the Russian parliament that a plane carrying the members of the self-styled State Emergency Committee, who attempted a coup d'etat on the night of 18-19 Aug., has landed at Simferopol Airport. The plane carrying Silayev, Bakatin, Primakov and Rutskoi is still en route to the Crimea.

Information received earlier by RIA on the suicide of Yazov has not been confirmed. RIA has since learned that Yazov, Pugo and two other members of the State Emergency Committee were on the first plane to the Crimea.

The Moscow White House has confirmed information on a proposed meeting between the Chief of the General Staff and Russian President Boris Yeltsin. The meeting seems likely to be held on Wednesday evening.

At a meeting of the presidium of the USSR Supreme Soviet earlier today it was decided to declare the coup unconstitutional.

## 17.07. ECHO OF MOSCOW ON THE AIR AGAIN

MOSCOW (RIA). At 3.30 this afternoon the radio station Echo of Moscow once more resumed broadcasting. This information was given to an RIA correspondent by the assistant editor-in-chief of Echo of Moscow, Sergei Fonton.

**17.12. ALL-UNION PUBLIC OPINION CENTRE SAYS PEOPLE CONDEMN THE COUP**

MOSCOW (RIA). On Aug. 20 the All-Union Public Opinion Centre carried out an opinion poll in various parts of the country on the political situation in the USSR. Of the 4,567 people asked their opinion 20% supported the actions of the State Emergency Committee, while 62% considered them illegal. In Russia and Kazakhstan 23% were for and 57% against. In the Ukraine 14% for and 72% against. Eighteen per cent believed the coming to power of the State Emergency Committee would result in an improvement of the country's economic situation, 50% believed it wouldn't. In the Ukraine 59% were pessimistic on this question, in Russia 47%, and in Kazakhstan 35%. Sixty per cent expected there would be mass repressions under the State Emergency Committee, 22% believed there wouldn't.

**17.36. EXTRAORDINARY SESSION OF MOSCOW CITY SOVIET TO BEGIN TOMORROW**

MOSCOW (RIA). At 10.00 tomorrow, Aug. 22, an extraordinary session of the Moscow City Soviet is to be held with ''The Political Situation in Moscow'' as the main point on the agenda. This information was given to an RIA correspondent by Andrei Bondarenko, a staffer at the Moscow Soviet press centre. Invitations have already been sent to Mayor of Moscow Gavril Popov, Prime Minister of the Moscow government Yuri Luzhkov, Moscow chiefs of the interior and KGB, the city prosecutor and Moscow deputies.

**17.45. ALL-UNION PUBLIC OPINION CENTRE SAYS PEOPLE OF MOSCOW AND YEREVAN BELIEVE STATE EMERGENCY COMMITTEE TO BE UNLAWFUL**

MOSCOW (RIA). Of the 1,792 Muscovites asked their opinion on the actions of the State Emergency Committee 73% considered them unlawful, while of the 155 people similarly asked in Yerevan 94% were of the same opinion. The opposite view was held by 13% in Moscow and 1% in Yerevan. Seventy-two per cent of Muscovites and 92 per cent of those asked in Yerevan expected mass repressions to ensue as a result of the coup. TOGLIATTI (PF). The press centres of the District Soviets in Togliatti have disseminated the Appeal of the Volga-Urals Military District to the citizens of Russia, which was signed by ''Officers, loyal to their oath''. In it the events of Aug. 19 are considered as the usurpation of power. The Appeal calls upon Russian officers not to use their weapons against the people, and retain their loyalty to their oath, to Russia and to President Yeltsin.

## 17.53. STATE EMERGENCY COMMITTEE MEMBERS AT GORBACHEV'S DACHA

MOSCOW (RIA). RIA has just learned from sources in the Kazakhstan parliament that the President of the Republic, Nursultan Nazarbayev, spoke today on the telephone to President Mikhail Gorbachev. The latter told him that he was still under guard by 30 KGB men, although his communications had been restored. The coup leaders were at his dacha in Foros and trying to get an audience with the President.

Nazarbayev implored Gorbachev under no circumstances to hold talks with the coup leaders, but to wait for the arrival of the delegation from Moscow, which included Russian leaders Ivan Silayev and Alexander Rutskoi and two members of the USSR Security Council, Vadim Bakatin and Yevgeni Primakov.

The Second Secretary of the CPSU Central Committee, Vladimir Ivashko, and the head of the Union Parliament, Anatoli Lukyanov, are also heading for the Crimea and should shortly arrive at Gorbachev's residence.

## 18.08. RESOLUTION OF MOSCOW CITY SOVIET PRESIDIUM ON TRAGIC EVENTS IN MOSCOW ON THE NIGHT OF 20-21 AUGUST, 1991

MOSCOW (RIA). The presidium of the Moscow City Soviet expressed deep condolences to the families of those who died on the night of Aug. 20-21 near the Sadovoye Ring Road. The presidium further decided to declare the day on which the dead should be buried a day of mourning throughout the City of Moscow and to provide material help for the bereaved families.

The Moscow Soviet presidium laid full blame for the deaths on those who gave orders for armed units to be sent into the city and demanded that the USSR Cabinet of Ministers withdraw from the city all troops not stationed in Moscow prior to Aug. 19. It was also decided to request that the Prosecutor of Moscow begin criminal proceedings in connection with the deaths.

According to information from the Mayor's press office three persons were killed: Vladimir Usov, aged 30; Dmitri Komar, aged 23; and one other man, so far unidentified. Another four persons received medical attention for bullet wounds of varying degrees of severity.

SVERDLOVSK (PF). A meeting was held earlier today at the Kalinin Machine Tools Factory, the director of which is Alexander Tizyakov, a member of the State Emergency Committee. The workers resolutely condemned "the actions of the unlawful committee and the unconstitutional coup carried out by them". The workers also sharply criticized the actions of their director.

18.22. SHAKHNAZAROV: MEMBERS OF STATE EMERGENCY COMMITTEE TO LEAVE THEIR POSTS

MOSCOW (RIA). The members of the State Emergency Committee will leave the posts they occupied in the country's administration before the coup, Georgi Shakhnazarov, a presidential aid, told an RIA correspondent. However, he was unable to say what measures in particular would be taken against the coup's organizers. He believed that it was more important at present to return all troops to the barracks, convene an extraordinary congress of the USSR People's Deputies and resolve several other specific issues.

Georgi Shakhnazarov could not say when the USSR President would return to Moscow and resume his responsibilities.

18.36. CHIEF ADMINISTRATION OF INTERIOR AND KGB FOR MOSCOW AND MOSCOW REGION ARE PLACED UNDER JURISDICTION OF RUSSIA

MOSCOW (RIA). According to the information of an RIA corespondent, the Chief Administration of the Interior and the KGB for Moscow and the Moscow Region have been placed under the jurisdiction of Russian authorities by a unanimous decision of the Russian Supreme Soviet. These structures were previously under the jurisdiction of the Union. The Russian KGB Chairman and Minister of the Interior are responsible for carrying out these measures within three days.

CHELYABINSK (PF). A freight car of state-of-the-art sub-machine guns equipped to take plastic bullets arrived at the Chelyabinsk Higher Military School of Automotive Engineering. The school's 17th company unloaded and accepted the weapons. According to unverified information, a special-purpose unit has been created at the school. Anatoly Zhezhera, the head of the school, said that this was routine replacement of old guns that had been planned back in 1990. Zhezhera refuted the report that the school had a special-purpose unit.

18.43. DJEMAL MIKELADZE REFUTES REPORT THAT GEORGIAN COMMUNIST PARTY SUPPORTS STATE EMERGENCY COMMITTEE

TBILISI (RIA). First Secretary of the Central Committee of the Independent Communist Party of Georgia Djemal Mikeladze refuted the report published in the newspaper Tskhovreba (Life) that the Georgian Communist Party supports the State Emergency Committee. According to him, at a closed Politburo meeting on Aug. 20 the discussion only concerned measures for maintaining law and order in Georgia as a result of the complicated situation in the country.

The Abkhazian Republican Committee of the Georgian Communist Party supported the activities of the State Emergency Committee. In a special statement published in Abkhazian newspapers, the authorities of the autonomous republic made no attempt to hide their delight with the coup. KAZAN (PF). On Aug. 21 the Bishop of Kazan and Mari Anastasi told a Postfactum correspondent that Orthodox priests were alarmed by the events occurring in the country but refrained from providing their parishioners with an interpretation of them, since the Russian Orthodox Church had not expressed its opinion about what had happened. According to Bishop Anastasi, "religious people are mainly concerned with their daily bread and are not very interested in politics, they are used to patiently enduring the tests which constantly fall to their lot".

**18.52.** MILITARY HELICOPTERS RETURN TO AIRFIELDS NEAR MOSCOW
MOSCOW (RIA). According to the general on duty at the Central Air Force Control Point, helicopters from military airfields in Chkalovsky and Peredelkino returned to their permanent stations.

**19.02.** SOLDIERS IN VILNIUS LEAVE FACILITIES THEY SEIZED
VILNIUS (RIA). Soldiers left the intercity telephone station in Vilnius they had seized several days ago. Earlier, soldiers left the Paneveshys and Siauliai radio and television retransmission stations they had seized during the night.

**19.14.** ARKADY VOLSKY ASKS CPSU TO CONDEMN THE COUP
MOSCOW (RIA). President of the USSR Scientific and Industrial Union, CPSU Central Committee member and USSR People's Deputy Arkady Volsky asked the CPSU Central Committee to condemn the coup in order to remove any suspicion from the party. At a press conference held on Aug. 21, he asked the republican leaders to immediately call a special meeting of the Federation Council with participation of USSR President Mikhail Gorbachev. Arkady Volsky asked the members of the USSR Security Council to carry out the tasks entrusted to them and take the necessary responsibility for coordinating measures to overcome the crisis and establish a legal government.

**19.20.** ADMINISTRATION OF CHIEF NAVY HEADQUARTERS SUPPORT YELTSIN
MOSCOW (RIA). Officers of the administration of the Chief Navy Headquarters asked USSR Minister of Defence Dmitry Yazov to withdraw from the State Emergency Committee and instruct the Armed Forces not to participate in political activities. They also asked their colleagues in administration agencies and headquarters of all levels to "follow the instructions of the only legal nationally elected leader at that moment--the Russian President."

## 19.46. GORBACHEV RETURNS TO MOSCOW

MOSCOW (RIA). According to the information of RIA, USSR President Mikhail Gorbachev left Simferopol this evening for Moscow. Russian Defence Minister Konstantin Kobets stated that "when he returns to Moscow President Gorbachev will receive an honourable welcome and the conspirators arrested".

## 19.32. BUSINESS RUSSIA BANK ORGANIZES COUP RELIEF FUND

MOSCOW (RIA). The collective of Business Russia Bank sent the following report through the RIA network:

Business Russia joint-stock bank has the honour of announcing the organization of a Coup Relief Fund.

The bank's collective has decided to make a contribution of one million roubles. For all those who care about the fate of their Homeland, the account number is:

116912 RCC Russian Central Bank in Moscow, Moscow Finance Department 201791, Business Russia Bank, Coup Relief Fund.

Authorized representatives of the RSFSR Supreme Soviet will have disposal of the money in this fund.

The names of organizations and persons who have taken active part in the formation of the fund will be announced regularly through the RIA network.

## 19.42. FUND FOR SUPPORTING DEFENDERS OF RUSSIAN PARLIAMENT BUILDING IS CREATED

MOSCOW (RIA). The association of joint ventures, international associations and organizations, the Union of Leaseholders, Business Men and Managers and the Bank and Stock-Exchange Association report that the attempted coup has taken a multi-million economic toll on the country, closed channels of foreign economic relations, curbed the import of new technology into the country and exacerbated the economic crisis which the putschists announced was their intention to overcome.

Last night these organizations created a one-and-a-half-million-rouble insurance fund to support the defenders of the White House at Krasnaya Presnya--the parliament and government of Russia. The same association and USSR Union of Leaseholders and Business Men decided to create a Fund for the Protection of the Russian Federation Constitution.

## 20.11. OFFICIAL DOCUMENT

MOSCOW (RIA). Appeal of the Russian Minister of Defence to the People of Moscow:

Dear Muscovites!

Thanks to your resolute support, we have defended Russia's sovereignty. The officers and personnel of military units who have been in the city during these days have shown restraint, have not succumbed to anticonstitutional appeals and have not permitted violence against the residents of the capital.

Now the troops are leaving Moscow and returning to their permanent stations. There is the possibility of armoured vehicles, tanks and other military technology breaking down as they leave the city.

I am appealing to you, Muscovites!

In the event of temporary halting during the movement of military columns, please refrain from any actions which could wound the dignity of our compatriots--the soldiers and officers. Show restraint and calm. Do not create conditions which will prevent troops from leaving the city.

I heartily thank all Muscovites for their support, courage and patriotism.

Glory to you, dear fellow countrymen!

*General Colonel Konstantin Kobets*
*21 August, 1991*

## 20.13. MEETING TO PROTECT GLASNOST IN MOSCOW

MOSCOW (RIA). At 17.00 a meeting was held to protect glasnost organized by the USSR Union of Journalists. It was held on Dzerzhinsky Square with the permission of the Moscow Soviet. Yegor Yakovlev, Vladimir Pozner, Alexander Yakovlev, Pavel Gusev and others spoke at the meeting, which was led by Chairman of the USSR Union of Journalists Eduard Sagalayev.

The demonstration was supposed to move on to Man<138>ge Square, but due to the great many people that gathered this proved impossible.

## 20.26. LIFE IN CAPITAL RETURNS TO NORMAL

MOSCOW (RIA). The special session of the Russian parliament which began on Aug. 21 has adjourned until Thursday. An agenda is to be adopted on 22 August.

Meanwhile, the mass meeting which has continued uninterrupted all day near the parliament building on Krasnopresnenskaya Embankment is still going on. Several thousand defenders of the "White House" decided to extend their vigil at the Parliament into the night. They began tearing down the barricades, but decided to leave one of them in place as a symbol of Muscovite endurance.

A meeting is also being held on Smolenskaya Square at the site of the tragic events of the night of Aug. 21 where three people were killed beneath the tanks. The obstructions have been torn down here, but battered trolleybuses still block traffic.

MOSCOW (PF). Despite the continuing withdrawal of troops from Moscow, there are still military units in the region of the ring-road. A company of armoured carriers (up to ten vehicles) is stationed at the crossroads of the ring-road and Dmitrov Highway. Near the Mytischi State Farm on the ring-road there are military units equipped to clean up the obstructions and barricades. Vehicles are circling to the north-east of the ring-road with soldiers in chemical defence uniform.

20.37. PACIFIC FLEET OBSERVES NEUTRALITY
VLADIVOSTOK (RIA). Acting chairman of the City Soviet Sergei Soloviev said at a City Soviet meeting that he had spoken by phone with the commander-in-chief of the Pacific Fleet, Vice-Admiral Gennady Khvatov. The admiral said that the Pacific sailors would observe neutrality. The crew of the large antisubmarine ship, the Tallinn, expressed their support of Russian President Boris Yeltsin.
TYUMEN (PF). On Aug. 21 a meeting of the bureau of the Tyumen CPSU Regional Committee was held at which the creation of the State Emergency Committee was recognized as anti-constitutional. The regional party leaders adopted this position only after the leaders of the CPSU Central Committee had made a similar statement. Earlier in an interview with the television news programme "Tyumen Meridian", First Secretary of the Tyumen CPSU Regional Committee Vladimir Chertischev said that consultations with lawyers had not confirmed that the creation of the State Emergency Committee contradicted the USSR Constitution. Tyumen Radio regularly broadcasts information about the activity of the Russian government. Representatives of democratic movements organized a picket at the building of the Tyumen Regional Soviet with slogans such as, "Freedom to Mikhail Gorbachev!", "Down with the imposters!", "The CPSU to court!"

20.46. MEETING IS PLANNED OF USSR PEOPLE'S DEPUTIES FROM NORTH-WESTERN RUSSIA AND THE BALTICS
LENINGRAD (RIA). On the initiative of Mayor of Leningrad Anatoly Sobchak a meeting of USSR Deputies from the Baltic and North-Western Russia is scheduled for 24 August. More than 400 Deputies have expressed their desire to attend the meeting. This will be their intermediate meeting before the session of the USSR Supreme Soviet to develop a joint position and plan of action. The Deputies plan to meet at the republican level on 25 August.

20.54. LANDSBERGIS' APPEAL TO CITIZENS OF LITHUANIA
VILNIUS (RIA). Chairman of the Supreme Soviet of Lithuania Vytautas Landsbergis asked the citizens of the republic to show goodwill towards Soviet soldiers and officers. As the Elta Agency reports, he noted that various kinds of "committee-ists" in the republic are trying to intimidate

and blackmail Soviet military personnel and spread slander and misinformation. "Let us show concern for our neighbours and tell the truth to those who have been misled about the strivings of the citizens of Lithuania and the actions of its administration," the chairman of the Lithuanian parliament said.

## 21.01. SECRETARIAT OF CPSU CENTRAL COMMITTEE CONDEMNS ATTEMPTED COUP

MOSCOW (RIA). "The Secretariat of the CPSU Central Committee, like all of society, has been placed under emergency conditions," a member of the Politburo and Secretary of the CPSU Central Committee Alexander Dzasokhov said on Aug. 21 at a press conference in Moscow. The party has had to give an evaluation of what happened postfactum. Dzasokhov read the statement of the Secretariat of the CPSU Central Committee which noted "the impermissibility of the use of an emergency situation by any political force or person whatsoever". The Secretariat of the Central Committee is in favour of an immediate review of the situation by the Supreme Soviet or Congress of the USSR People's Deputies, as well as the immediate convening of a Plenum of the CPSU Central Committee with the participation of Mikhail Gorbachev.

"We have turned out to be hostages of a war between Union and Russian laws," said Secretary of the CPSU Central Committee Vladimir Kalashnikov, who took part in the press conference, to explain the fact that the CPSU did not give its opinion of the coup until the third day. "Could we have immediately condemned this action unequivocally? We needed time to come to terms with it."

Vladimir Kalashnikov responded in the negative when an RIA corespondent asked whether it was true that the official position of the Secretariat of the CPSU Central Committee had only appeared after it was clear that the coup had failed.

KYZYL (PF). The command of the Kyzyl military garrison prevented meetings between deputies and officers. Chairman of the Kyzyl City Soviet Yuri Slobodchikov said that they gave the orders and instructions from the command of the Siberian Military District as the reason for their refusal. The Kyzyl City Soviet in its address "To the residents of Tuva" described the members of the State Emergency Committee as "imposters and mutineers". The Kyzyl City Soviet decided not to ask citizens to strike, however the Soviet promised to support those enterprises who began to strike. The Supreme Soviet of the Tuva Autonomous Republic took a wait-and-see attitude and did not adopt any documents concerning the events going on in the country. The republican administration of the KGB announced its subordination to Kryuchkov and the republic's public prosecutor's office, its subordination to the USSR Public Prosecutor's Office, while the Tuva Ministry of the Interior supports the Russian administration. The newspaper of the Tuva Republic's committee of the CPSU, Tuvinskaya pravda, refused to publish the decrees and addresses of the Russian President and instructions from the Russian government. The republican committee for television and radio broadcasting refused to give air time to democratically oriented Deputies of the Russian Federation and Kyzyl City Soviet. The republican military recruitment office began mobilizing reserves "to gathering harvests". Increased combat readiness has been declared in the units of the Kyzyl garrison since Aug. 19.

IRKUTSK (PF). Chairman of the Irkutsk Regional Executive Committee Yuri Nozhikov said that, according to unverified sources, troops are moving from Chita and Buryatia towards Irkutsk.

BRATSK (PF). On Aug. 21 at a meeting of the presidium of the Bratsk City Soviet the enterprises of Bratsk decided to go on strike only if troops entered the city. It was also decided to ask the leaders of the local subdivisions of the Interior Ministry and KGB to subordinate themselves only to the corresponding leading agencies of Russia, ignoring all instructions from the State Emergency Committee.

## 21.30 DEMANDS

of the Russian President on the organizers of the anticonstitutional coup
To Gennadi Yanaev, Oleg Baklanov, Vladimir Kryuchkov, Valentin Pavlov, Boris Pugo, Vassili Starodubtsev, Alexandr Tizyakov and Dmiri Yazov
Aware of my responsibility for the future of the Homeland and taking as a basis the political self-expression of the citizens of Russia, I make the following demands on you:

1. I order the State Emergency Committee to cease their illegal anticonstitutional activity from 22.00 on Aug. 21 1991. All decisions made from the moment of its formation are subjected to unqualified repeal.

2. I oblige the committee to immediately repeal all decisions which prevent USSR President Mikhail Gorbachev from carrying out his constitutional responsibilities.

3. In the event that these demands are not met, I will adopt all measures stipulated by the Law to stop the illegal activity of the committee and ensure constitutional law and order in the country.

*President of the Russian Federation Boris Yeltsin*
*21 August 1991*

21.43  RUSSIAN PRESIDENTIAL DECREE No. 70
ON REMOVING THE CHAIRMEN OF EXECUTIVE COMMITTEES
OF TERRITORIAL AND REGIONAL SOVIETS OF RUSSIAN PEO-
PLE'S DEPUTIES FROM THEIR RESPONSIBILITIES
       For supporting the anticonstitutional activity of the so-called State
Emergency Committee and not carrying out the decrees of the Russian
President directed at stopping the coup and based on Articles 121-128 of the
Russian Federation Constitution and Article 8 of the Russian Federation
Law on "The Russian Federation President", I decree that:
       1. The following people be removed from their posts as executive
committee chairmen:
N.I. Goroviy (Krasnodar Territory);
V.V. Borodaev (Rostovs Region);
V.L. Tarkhov (Samara Region);
V.F. Toporkov (Lipetsk Region).
       2. The Public Prosecutor's Office, Ministry of the Interior and State
Security Committee (KGB) of the Russian Federation conduct an investi-
gation of the activity of the above-mentioned people.
President of the Russian Federation Boris Yeltsin

*Moscow, Kremlin*
*21 August 1991*


21.56  RUSSIAN FEDERATION PRESIDENTIAL DECREE No. 69
ON THE MASS MEDIA IN THE RUSSIAN FEDERATION
       A group of persons declaring themselves to be the State Emergency
Committee have established control over the mass media and created a
special agency, in essence carrying out the function of political censor. They
have also closed several democratic publications. The All-Union Television
and Radio Broadcasting Company has essentially become one of the main
instruments in carrying out the anti-constitutional coup. Thus, an attempt
has been made to repeal the USSR Law on the Press and Other Mass Media.
As a result of these actions, freedom of speech, as a genuine achievement
of democracy, has been placed under serious threat.
       Under these circumstances, I decree that:
       1. The decisions issued by the state of emergency committee with
respect to the mass media be repealed as invalid from the moment of their
issue.
       2. The propaganda of the decisions of the State Emergency Commit-
tee be banned as activity directed towards support of the government coup
in the USSR.

3. Chairman of the All-Union Television and Radio Broadcasting Company Leonid Kravchenko be removed from his duties, and the RSFSR Public Prosecutor's Office be entrusted with the legal evaluation of his activities until the USSR President can resolve the issue.

4. The All-Union Television and Radio Broadcasting Company be placed under the authority of the Russian Government.

Leadership of the All-Union Television and Radio Broadcasting Company be temporarily placed under the authority of the Russian Federation Minister for Press and Mass Media Mikhail Poltoranin until a chairman is appointed to it in accordance with the legislation.

5. The second all-union television channel be placed under the authority of the Russian State Television and Radio Broadcasting Company to create a republican television network.

6. The Russian Federation Ministry for Press and Mass Media and the administration of the All-Union Television and Radio Broadcasting Company be responsible for ensuring the functioning of the mass media on the territory of the Russian Federation in accordance with the USSR Law on the Press and Other Mass Media.

7. The leaders of all forms of mass media of the Russian Federation be responsible for efficient provision of the population with information about the decisions of the Supreme Soviet, President and government of the Russian Federation.

8. This Decree is effective from the moment it is signed.

President of the Russian Federation Boris Yeltsin

*Moscow, Kremlin*
*21 August 1991*

## 22.39. USSR PRESIDENT HAS STILL NOT ARRIVED IN MOSCOW

MOSCOW (RIA). Mikhail Gorbachev is expected to arrive in Moscow around midnight, after which he may go to the USSR Ministry of Foreign Affairs Press Centre for a meeting with journalists.

According to the air traffic control service at Vnukovo Airport, the President's airplane had still not arrived at 22.00 Moscow time.

## 22.46. THE SECRETARIAT OF THE KARABAKH COMMITTEE APPEALS TO THE RUSSIAN AUTHORITIES TO PUT AN END TO THE VIOLENCE IN NAGORNO-KARABAKH

MOSCOW (RIA). On Aug. 21, the Secretariat of the Karabakh Committee of Russian Intelligentsia sent a telegram to the Supreme Soviet, President and Vice-President of Russia asking for an end to be put to the onslaught of violence in Nagorno-Karabakh and for the military leadership guilty of murder, deportation, the seizing of hostages, torture, derision and violation of the rights of the Armenian people to be committed to trial. An offensive against democracy has been launched in Nagorno-Karabakh and bloody rehearsals of the military coup in Moscow have been carried out, the telegram said.

ALMA-ATA. Press secretary to the President of the Kazakh Republic Gailbek Shalakhmetov said that Kazakhstan President Nursultan Nazarbayev talked by phone with USSR Vice-President Gennady Yanayev had spoken to each other by phone. The Kazakhstan President directly asked the latter whether there were plans to storm the Russian parliament and arrest Russian President Yeltsin. Nazarbayev particularly stressed that this step was categorically impermissible.

22.49. USSR CABINET OF MINISTERS DID NOT TAKE ANY ACTION DURING COUP SINCE IT COMPLETELY TRUSTED ITS ORGANIZERS

MOSCOW (RIA). The USSR Cabinet of Ministers did not take any action during the attempted military coup on 19-21 August because it completely trusted its organizers, Vladimir Shcherbakov, first USSR deputy prime minister, announced at a press conference. According to him, the government, being an executive body, could not, in contrast to the Russian legislative agencies, interfere in events, all the more so since "like other Soviet citizens" it only had information about them from the broadcasts of Central Television and the newspapers allowed by the State Emergency Committee.

Responding to a question from an RIA correspondent about why the Cabinet was not taking advantage of the reports of the small number of agencies who were continuing to work during these days, Shcherbakov said that they were not always sufficiently accurate. He also explained his inaction by the fact that according to the Constitution, in the event that the USSR President is unable to fulfil has responsibilities, power is transferred to the vice-president. However, the government was unable to achieve confirmation from Gennady Yanayev and Anatoly Lukyanov concerning the constitutionality of their actions.

22.53. SHCHERBAKOV: RESIGNATION OF CABINET OF MINISTERS WOULD BE "TREASON WITH RESPECT TO COUNTRY'S POPULATION"

MOSCOW (RIA). The USSR Cabinet of Ministers does not intend to resign, although this issue was raised at its meeting today, said First USSR Deputy Prime Minister Vladimir Shcherbakov at the press conference. "This would be treason with respect to the country's population in the current extremely difficult situation," he said.

Shcherbakov read a statement from the Cabinet of Ministers adopted today at a meeting of its presidium. The government intends to be guided by the USSR Constitution and carry out the decisions of the country's administration. It sees its main task under current conditions as ensuring law and order and the freedoms of citizens, as well as stabilizing the economic situation in the country. The Cabinet of Ministers is also asking the heads of governments and international economic organizations not to cease economic relations with the USSR as constitutional order will soon be restored. Shcherbakov also said that the government has created a group which will investigate the events of recent days. The USSR Public Prosecutor's Office has also been given these instructions.

As for Valentin Pavlov's illness, Shcherbakov said that he really is in a serious state. He also said that the prime minister did not know anything about preparations for the coup.

23.35. ATTEMPTED COUP IN THE USSR--REASONS AND CONSEQUENCES: VIEW OF A SOCIOLOGIST
MOSCOW (RIA). On Aug. 20 1991 almost half (47 per cent) of the 4,567 people surveyed were unable to answer the question, "Do you think that now only amoral politicians can appeal for social confrontation?", reports news agency Data with reference to a All-Union Public Opinion Centre survey. Eleven per cent of those surveyed did not find anything criminal in this kind of appeal.

23.40. YAZOV HAS LEFT FOR PARTS UNKNOWN
MOSCOW (RIA). According to unverified data, on Aug. 21 at 14.30 an airplane carrying Dmitry Yazov left Moscow's Vnukovo Airport. The flight's destination is unknown.

23.45. ROUND TABLE MEETING AT MOSCOW SOVIET
MOSCOW (RIA). On Aug. 21 a round table meeting of political parties and   movements was held at the Moscow Soviet at which questions were discussed associated with the attempted coup in the USSR.

It was the democratic forces who defended the constitutional structure, the institution of presidency and the USSR President himself, noted former member of the Politburo of the CPSU Central Committee and now chairman of the city assembly of Moscow Alexander Yakovlev. No one is guilty of what happened but the President for surrounding himself with those types of people, he stressed. In his opinion the time has come to get rid of people who have been driving us into an impasse these past six years. The round table meeting also stressed the need to conduct an investigation of the activity of all the participants in the attempted coup.

## 23.51. DEPARTIZATION IN KYRGYZSTAN

BISHKEK (RIA). According to the report of IMA-Press on the morning of Aug. 21 President of Kyrgyzstan Askar Akayev issued decrees concerning the departization of the republic's KGB and Ministry of the Interior agencies, the privatization of party property and ceasing of the activity of the Communist Party of Kyrgyzstan.

This occurred after the republic's Communist Party supported the Gang of Eight, while Akayev stated that the creation of the State Emergency Committee was an unconstitutional step.

## 00.30. LENINGRAD SOVIET KEEPS VIGIL

LENINGRAD (RIA). Late in the evening of Aug. 21 a decision was made at a meeting of the headquarters for emergency situation of the Leningrad City Soviet to maintain guard at Mariinsky Palace where the Leningrad Soviet is located. The Leningrad Soviet will work all night. At 22.00 representatives of committees for the support of Soviet power, which had been formed at enterprises, arrived at Mariinsky Palace. They announced their willingness to act in accordance with the instructions of the Leningrad Soviet headquarters. The headquarters' next meeting will take place on 22 August at 9 a.m. and a press conference is planned for 3 p.m. At the request of a correspondent from the newspaper Vecherny Leningrad, Mayor of Leningrad Anatoli Sobchak commented on the statement made by anchorman of the Leningrad TV programme "600 Seconds" Alexander Nevzorov that the coup of 19 August was "staged". "I have learned from experience that it is not worth creating a scene around this person," said Sobchak. "His statements are his own personal conjectures. I don't think it could have been a farce because we have been through two very distressing nights."

## 00.49. RUSSIAN LEADERS AND USSR PRESIDENT FLY TO MOSCOW

MOSCOW (RIA). At 00.04 Moscow time on 22 August the Russian administration's TU-134 aircraft left the Crimea for Moscow carrying Rutskoi, Silayev and USSR President Mikhail Gorbachev. The administration of Vnukovo Airport reported that the president's aircraft is expected to land at Vnukovo-2 Airport at 01.30.

RIA managed to obtain a chronicle of the flights of the government aircraft on 21 August between Moscow and the Crimes:

14.18. IL-62 with members of the emergency committee on board left the technical base at Vnukovo. The aircraft took off several minutes before the arrival of a group of 50 policemen from the Russian Interior Ministry who had been sent to arrest the committee members.

16.08. A similar aircraft without passengers took off from Vnukovo-2.

16.52. TU-134 took off from Vnukovo-2 for Foros, on board were Alexander Rutskoi, Ivan Silayev and Vadim Bakatin. However, it was denied permission to land under the pretext that an airplane had recently landed at the same airport and broken an undercarriage. Passengers notified Boris Yeltsin of this, and he then negotiated with Navy Commander, Admiral Chernavin, who gave permission to land.

20.00. IL-62 took off from Vnukovo-2 (aircraft number 86712)--the USSR President's aircraft. At 21.55 it landed on Foros Cape.

The same sources said that the USSR President signed a decree concerning the arrest of the junta members and refused to receive them at his dacha in the Crimea.

## 0.19. "ROCK AT THE BARRICADES" NEAR RUSSIAN PARLIAMENT BUILDING

MOSCOW (RIA). A concert which lasted more than three hours, called "Rock at the Barricades" was held on Krasnopresnenskaya Embankment near the Russian parliament building. Such groups as the Time Machine, Kruiz, Shakh and Korroziya Metalla performed at the concert. Nikolai Karachentsov, who also performed at the concert, said that actors from the Lenin Komsomol Moscow Theatre cancelled their evening performance on 21 August and came to the White House to support its defenders.

## 02.56. PRECAUTIONARY MEASURES ARE TIGHTENED AT THE RUSSIAN HOUSE OF SOVIETS

MOSCOW (RIA). Precautionary measures have been tightened at the Russian parliament building. A guard explained to an RIA correspondent that this was done to remove any extraneous persons from the building.

## 02.58. ALEXANDER RUTSKOI: USSR PRESIDENT IN MOSCOW, "VILLAIN KRYUCHKOV HAS BEEN ARRESTED"

MOSCOW (RIA). "The Russian police is assuming sole responsibility for the protection and safety of the USSR President's flight," chief of the Russian transportation police Maj. Gen. Kulikov told an RIA correspondent. However, some of the USSR President's guards were on duty at the check-in point at Vnukovo-2 Airport. One of them, who refused to give his name, said that no one had yet abolished his department. "The police," he stressed, "always participates in such measures."

One of the President's guards also stated that he did not know if the KGB chief Vladimir Kryuchkov was still his boss.

In an interview to the "White House RAdio", Alexander Rutskoi stated that "villain Kryuchkov" has been arrested and turned over to the Russian Ministry of the Interior".

04.28. IVAN SILAYEV: UNION TREATY COULD BE SIGNED BY
BEGINNING OF OCTOBER

MOSCOW (RIA). "Sixty per cent" of the junta members who
attempted an anticonstitutional coup in the USSR have been arrested,
Russian Prime Minister Ivan Silayev told a group of journalists.

According to Silayev, Mikhail Gorbachev warmly thanked the
Russian delegation for coming and expressed dismay at the activity of the
conspirators. During the last few days he had been essentially isolated from
the world and deprived of the opportunity to read the newspapers or obtain
information from the radio or television.

Responding to a multitude of journalists' questions, Ivan Silayev said
he was convinced that the recent events would not have a significantly
negative effect on the country's foreign policy. At the same time, he stressed
that internal reforms would now be carried out more radically and "with a
different team of performers, of course".

According to Silayev, a Union Treaty could be signed by the end of
September or beginning of October.

Ivan Silayev also said that the USSR President would speak at the
session of the Russian Supreme Soviet.

10.01. USSR INTERIOR MINISTER BORIS PUGO SHOOTS HIM-
SELF?

MOSCOW (RIA). According to information received by RIA from
reliable sources, one of the members of the so-called State Emergency
Committee, USSR Interior Minister Boris Pugo has committed suicide. His
body was found by representatives of law-enforcement agencies who had
come to arrest him. He shot himself with a standard pistol.

10.06. THE TELEVISION AND RADIO CENTRES OF ESTONIA AND
LATVIA ARE FREED

MOSCOW (RIA). The news agencies of the Baltic republics report
the following:

TALLINN. At 19.00 on 21 August the military left the Tallinn
television tower, seized by the that morning, after two-hour negotiations
between Estonian Prime Minister Edgar Savisaar and military leaders who
had heard about the failure of the coup.

RIGA. On 21 August "White Berets", the government police of
Latvia, released the television and radio centre seized by OMON on Aug.
19. The television and radio centre sustained serious material damage, not
only was equipment ruined, but door-plates were also smashed.

10.11. LATVIA: OMON IS ASKED TO CONFESS THEIR GUILT

RIGA (RIA). The Presidium of the Latvian Supreme Soviet asked the
OMON soldiers who participated in violent acts during the "state of

emergency'' to voluntarily turn themselves over to the republic's public prosecutor's office. A confession of guilt will be considered an extenuating circumstance, the presidium's statement said. This was reported by the Baltia agency.

10.45. PARTICIPANTS OF CONGRESS OF EXPATRIATES CONDEMN ATTEMPTED COUP
MOSCOW (RIA). On the evening of Aug. 21 participants in the International Congress of Expatriates sent a letter to the Russian and USSR presidents, as well as to the UN Secretary General, in which they condemned the "putschists headed by Yanayev". "It is obvious that the Communists do not have enough of that blood which they have been spilling since 1917," the letter said. "We came to our ancestors' homeland to share knowledge, talents and experience with our fellow-countrymen which could be useful on the road to rebirth of our Fatherland, but instead we have been forced to think of security measures for our ancestors' Fatherland at the gun point of tanks and armoured carried." The authors of the letter called the attempted coup an attempt to drive the people under the yoke of the Communist Party by force.

11.08. LITHUANIAN PRIME MINISTER IS PLEASED BY GORBACHEV'S RETURN
VILNIUS (RIA). Lithuanian Prime Minister Gyadiminas Vagnorius sent a telegram to Mikhail Gorbachev in which he expressed genuine delight that he had again resumed his responsibilities as USSR President, reports the Baltia agency. The prime minister hopes that the victory of progressive forces and Gorbachev's personal position will aid normalization of relations between Lithuania and the USSR and precipitate constructive inter-government negotiations.

11.16. IVAN SILAYEV CALLS LUKYANOV "THE IDEOLOGICAL MASTERMIND OF THE PLOT"
MOSCOW (RIA). Chairman of the USSR Supreme Soviet Anatoli Lukyanov in essence was the "junta's main ideologue, the ideological mastermind of the plot," said Russian Prime Minister Ivan Silayev on 22 August at a session of the republican parliament. Talking before the deputies, he said that he was finally persuaded of this yesterday during a meeting between Lukyanov and Gorbachev which he attended. "It was disgusting to watch how he humiliatingly justified his inaction, making an attempt to mislead us. I do not believe him," said Ivan Silayev.

## 11.20. BORIS YELTSIN'S SPEECH AT SESSION OF RUSSIAN SUPREME SOVIET

MOSCOW (RIA). Hospitalized Valentin Pavlov has been placed under guard, and some of the putschists have been arrested, announced Russian President Boris Yeltsin when he spoke at the session of the Russian Supreme Soviet. In addition, he informed those gathered of Ivan Silayev's trip to the Crimea and Gorbachev's return to Moscow. Yeltsin reported that the heads of all the reading states of the world had phoned him recently and noted Russia's role in protecting the process of democratization.

Yeltsin also reported that several chairmen of regional executive committees have been removed from their posts for recognizing the authority of the Emergency Committee and carrying out its decisions.

Boris Yeltsin thanked the Muscovites who maintained all-round defence at the Russian parliament building for three days.

## 11.33. THE SQUARE AT THE RUSSIAN PARLIAMENT IS NAMED FREE RUSSIA SQUARE

MOSCOW (RIA). Boris Yeltsin will appear on the balcony of the Russian parliament building at noon to inform the participants of the meeting which has been taking place there of the republican administration's position on currently important questions.

It is also apparent that the square adjacent to the Russian parliament will soon be given a new official name. The Muscovites who defended the Russian White House propose that it be called Free Russia Square. At this side, the former epicentre of barricade fighting during the 1905 revolution, barricades were once more erected to prevent a possible storm of the parliament.

## 11.58. PUTSCHISTS ARRESTED, BORIS PUGO SHOOTS HIMSELF

MOSCOW (RIA). At the special session of the Russian Supreme Soviet currently in progress, a representative of the Public Prosecutor's Office of the Russian Federation stated that criminal proceedings began yesterday against all members of the "Gang of Eight" who undertook the coup d'etat. He confirmed the arrest of Kryuchkov, Yazov and Tizyakov yesterday after they arrived from Foros, and also reported that a group had been sent today to arrest former USSR Interior Minister Pugo. However, when the group tried to enter the apartment, Pugo shot himself. He also reported that the Russian Public Prosecutor's Office had only just finished searching the office of USSR Vice-President Yanayev, and Yanayev himself was at present being questioned by the Russian Public Prosecutor's Office which will carry out the investigation.

According to certain sources, a member of the Emergency Committee Oleg Baklanov was arrested but then released since he is at present a

USSR People's Deputy. He will be detained after the USSR Supreme Soviet comes to a decision concerning deprivation of his deputy's immunity. Vassili Starodubtsev has left Moscow and measure are being taken to arrest him.

## 12.07. ARMENIAN LEADERS EXPRESS DELIGHT AT THE ACTIVITY OF THE RUSSIAN ADMINISTRATION

YEREVAN (RIA). Leaders of the Armenian Republic Levon Ter-Petrosyan and Vazgen Manukyan sent a letter to Russian leaders Boris Yeltsin, Ruslan Khasbulatov and Ivan Silayev on Aug. 21 in which they expressed their delight at the actions of the Russian administration which was able to prevent the establishment of an anticonstitutional regime capable of plunging the country into a bloody civil war.

The previous evening, the Presidium of the Supreme Soviet of the Armenian Republic made a statement in which it expressed its opposition to violence, announced the State of Emergency Committee incompetent and called for an immediate convening of the USSR Federation Council to stabilize the situation in the country.

## 12.11. PUBLICATION AND DISSEMINATION OF SEVERAL NEWSPAPERS IS SUSPENDED IN LITHUANIA

VILNIUS (RIA). In Lithuania the publication and dissemination of more than twenty newspapers has been temporarily suspended. Among them are all the national newspapers permitted by the Emergency Committee, as well as several local ones, Litva sovetskaya, Taribu Letuva, Sovetskaya Klaipeda and several others. This was done on the basis of Article 3 of the Treaty "On the Fundamental Principles of Inter-Government Relations" between Lithuania and Russia and Article 6 of the Law on Mass Media of the Lithuanian Republic, which bans the dissemination of information which sows discord and stirs up ethnic strife.

## 12.29. SECURITY COUNCIL SET UP IN KAZAKHSTAN

ALMA ATA (RIA). Kazakhstan President Nursultan Nazarbayev signed a Decree on the Formation of a Republican Security Council, which includes, besides himself, the heads of the Interior Ministry and KGB, the commander of border troops and the Mayor of Alma Ata. The commander-in-chief of the army stationed in Kazakhstan is not a member of the Council since he supported the Emergency Committee. The purpose of the new republican agency is to protect the Kazakhstan Constitution. According to certain reports, there is talk in the republic's corridors of power of the need to create their own armed units to oppose any attempts to remove legally elected authorities in an emergency situation.

RIA was informed that during the coup Nazarbayev had issued a secret order in Kazakhstan which banned any troop movement around the republic.

### 12.44. LEADERS OF SOVIET AUTHORITIES OF KAMCHATKA LEAVE CPSU

PETROPAVLOVSK-KAMCHATSKY (RIA). Chairman of the Kamchatka Regional Soviet Pyotr Permyak and Chairman of the Kamchatka Regional Executive Committee Vladimir Biryukov announced their intention to leave the CPSU. In an interview with an RIA correspondent both leaders said that they considered it impossible to be members of the Communist Party, the ruling clique of which had orchestrated the coup. In their words, the Kamchatka Regional Committee of the CPSU had put pressure on them to support the putschists. Chairman of the local television and radio broadcasting committee Valeri Martynenko said that the regional CPSU committee had banned, for example, the broadcasts of the only independent television company on the peninsula to report reliable information from Moscow during the coup.

### 13.03. PRESIDENT SHAIMIYEV'S POSITION DURING THE COUP IS NOT INCLUDED ON AGENDA OF TATAR PARLIAMENT

KAZAN (RIA). Three issues were included on the agenda marked for the Aug. 27 session of the Tatar Supreme Soviet: the state emblem and flag and the corresponding changes in the republic's constitution. The position of Tatar President Mintimer Shaimiyev, who supported the State Emergency Committee and ordered that all its instructions be carried out in the republic, will not be officially discussed. However, it is reported that the democratic factions would insist that this issue be put on the agenda.

A special meeting of the Kazan City Soviet and Executive Committee will be held on Aug. 24 to discuss this issue. Source in the Tatar capital report that the meeting will raise the question on confidence in the republic's president.

### 13.49. MASS MEETING ON MOSCOW'S KRASNOPRESNENSKAYA EMBANKMENT

MOSCOW (RIA). The abortive coup be the so-called State Emergency Committee was sanctioned by the neo-Stalinist nucleus in the CPSU Central Committee, said Boris Yeltsin. Speaking at a meeting at the Russian parliament building on Aug. 22 he said that any further activity of the Russian Communist Party, which had still not been registered, should not be allowed. He called Anatoli Lukyanov the "ideological mastermind of the coup".

The Russian President stated that the republic's Supreme Soviet had decided to make the white-azure-red banner the state flag of Russia.

In his speech at the meeting Ivan Silayev state that a proposal had been made at the Russian Supreme Soviet to reinstate the St. George Cross award and institute new Russian decorations, the first holders of which should be those who resisted the coup.

Ruslan Khasbulatov told the meeting that he made a proposal concerning nationalization of the building of the CPSU Central Committee on Staraya Square. He also suggested reviewing the issue concerning the newspapers Sovetskaya Rossiya and Rabochaya tribuna which had taken up the slogans of the mutineers. According to Khasbulatov, journalists should dismiss the leaders of these newspapers and their collectives should take control of the printing house.